100 BEST FOODS FOR MENOPAUSE

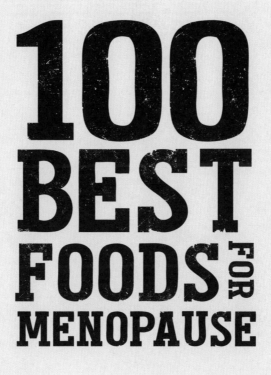

100 BEST FOODS FOR MENOPAUSE

This edition published by Parragon Books Ltd in 2015 and distributed by

Parragon Inc.
440 Park Avenue South, 13th Floor
New York, NY 10016
www.parragon.com/lovefood

LOVE FOOD is an imprint of Parragon Books Ltd

ISBN 978-1-4748-1173-6

Printed in China

Created and produced by Ivy Contract
Consultant: Judith Wills
New photography by Clive Streeter

Notes for the Reader
This book uses standard kitchen measuring spoons and cups. All spoon and cup measurements are level unless otherwise indicated. Unless otherwise stated, milk is assumed to be whole, eggs are large, individual vegetables are medium, pepper is freshly ground black pepper, and salt is table salt. Unless otherwise stated, all root vegetables should be peeled prior to using.

For best results, use a food thermometer when cooking meat. Check the latest government guidelines for current advice.

Cover photograph by Max and Liz Haarala Hamilton

CONTENTS

INTRODUCTION

When a woman enters her late forties or early fifties—or, occasionally, earlier or later than this—her body goes through various far-reaching physical changes, as her ovulation and periods gradually stop. The months or years before the periods cease completely is called the perimenopause, while the time when they stop is the official menopause. The years following are termed postmenopausal, although many women continue to experience some of the symptoms associated with peri- and menopausal times, and they feel that they are still, practically speaking, going through menopause.

Symptoms of menopause include physical ones, such as hot flashes—a feeling of unbearable heat, reddening, and perhaps sweating—night sweats, insomnia, tiredness, headaches; plus general aches and pains, forgetfulness, and dry skin. They may also include emotional problems, such as anxiety, depression, mood swings, or tearfulness. Many of these symptoms are the result of the somewhat sudden and dramatic drop in levels of the hormone estrogen in the body.

While some women choose to try hormone replacement therapy (HRT) to deal with menopause, a lot of the symptoms can be improved considerably simply by making lifestyle changes. Getting regular exercise and fresh air, and pacing yourself are helpful—but perhaps the most can be achieved through the right diet

choices. What and how we eat can make a big difference to our health and well-being before, during, and after the menopausal years.

Eating through menopause

During menopause and afterward, we now know that there are many foods—all of which are featured in this book—that have specific, positive effects on your health and well-being because of the particular nutrients and/or chemicals they contain. Some can help to minimize hot flashes or insomnia, for example, while others may improve your mood or lift depression. There are foods that can improve dry skin and others that will help you beat tiredness. In fact, whatever the menopausal symptom, there is a food that can help. If you choose from this food list regularly, you can make a real difference to how you feel, your quality of life, and your future life.

The general rules of healthy eating for adults still apply in the menopausal years. These, in brief are:

• Eat at least five portions of fruit and vegetables a day (seven is better). Be sure you have both fruit and vegetables—not all fruit, for example. Eat a rainbow of fruit and vegetables in different colors, and choose from different types of vegetables (such as leafy greens, root vegetables, beans) and fruits (fruit with pits, berries, citrus fruit, exotic fruit), so that you get a wide variety of all the beneficial chemicals and compounds in the different types.
• Eat adequate protein—lean meat, poultry, seafood, fish, eggs, low-fat dairy produce, nuts, seeds, and beans, for example. Include oily fish in your diet at least two to three times a week.
• Eat complex carbohydrates instead of simple types—for example, choose whole-grain or whole-wheat bread, whole-grain cereals for breakfast, and brown rice and whole-wheat pasta instead of the highly refined white types. Keep your intake of sugar and other sweeteners low.
• Include a moderate amount of fat in your diet, but make it monounsaturated fat (such as olive oil) or other healthy oils most of the time. Cut down on saturated fats, such as those in whole milk and other dairy and fatty meat, and trans fats, which are used in baked goods, snacks, and margarines.
• Try to eat a natural diet; avoid packaged and canned goods or highly refined processed foods.
• For women, keep alcohol intake to one glass a day, and have two alcohol-free days a week.

Menopause, food, and your future

One of the consequences of the drop in hormone levels experienced during menopause is that women begin to lose bone density, and at a rapid rate. This is the main cause of osteoporosis in later life. Another consequence is that women's incidence of cardiovascular disease increases to the same level as men's, because the female hormones no longer offer the protection against the disease that they did before. Weight gain and type 2 diabetes also become much more common during and after menopause, because it appears our metabolic rate takes a dip, while hormonal changes mean the body is more predisposed to put on fat around the waist and abdomen. Many women also report a loss of libido.

The good news is that making the right food choices before, during, and after menopause can make a huge difference, benefitting us not only at the time, but also in the long-term. Even the risk of some types of cancer that commonly affect us in late middle age or old age can be minimized through what we eat. It's important to get into the habit of doing all you can now to limit the negative effects of this change in life—by eating a vitamin D-, calcium-, and magnesium-rich diet for your bones, for example; by choosing foods that help to lower cholesterol and blood pressure for your heart, and that protect you from cancer; and by choosing healthy foods that satisfy your appetite without contributing too many calories.

The following pages will tell you all you need to know about which foods can help you the most, now and in the years ahead.

1

Fruits

Fresh fruit is an excellent food for weight control during menopause, and is a source of several nutrients—including vitamin C, a range of antioxidants, and fiber—which have a positive effect on menopausal symptoms. Dried fruit is a valuable addition to the diet, providing high levels of minerals and fibers.

(W) Ideal for weight control

(F) High in fiber

(B) Protects and strengthens bones

(H) Heart health

(M) Mood booster

(S) Improves skin condition

01 APPLES

Apples are one of the best fruits you can eat during menopause. They contain a significant number of compounds that have positive benefits for health and well-being throughout life.

Apples are also ideal for dieters because they are low in calories, virtually fat-free, and keep hunger at bay by releasing the hormone GLP-1 (glucagon-like peptide), which sends "I'm full" signals to the brain. Although they are not rich in vitamins and minerals—apart from vitamin C, which helps to boost mood and brain function, and potassium, which helps minimize fluid retention—apples are an excellent source of plant chemicals, including quercetin, which may protect against Alzheimer's disease. The peel contains ursolic acid, a compound that helps maintain muscle bulk and prevent weight gain. The ursolic acid, along with the soluble fiber pectin and the compound D-glucaric acid in the fruit itself, also helps to lower cholesterol. Red-skinned apples contain anthocyanins, pigments that help improve memory and brain function.

• Rich in plant compounds that keep the heart healthy.
• Vitamin C improves brain function and mood.
• Pectin and acids help improve our cholesterol profile.
• A good source of potassium, which helps prevent fluid retention.

Practical tips:
Store apples in the crisper compartment of the refrigerator or in a cool, dark place, because light and heat destroy vitamins and compounds. Wash before eating, but don't peel them because the skin contains up to five times as many plant chemicals as the flesh.

DID YOU KNOW?

In general, old varieties of apple, such as Pippin and Granny Smith, contain less fructose (sugar) than newer varieties, such as Pink Lady and Fuji. Red-skinned apples tend to contain more of the beneficial compounds.

MAJOR NUTRIENTS PER AVERAGE-SIZE APPLE (4 oz.)

Calories	60
Total fat	Trace
Protein	Trace
Carbohydrate	16 g
Fiber	2.8 g
Vitamin C	5 mg
Potassium	123 mg

Waldorf salad

SERVES 4   (**W**) (**B**) (**H**)

½ cup pecans

4 apples, such as Cortland,
   Empire, or Red Delicious

juice of 1 lemon

4 celery stalks, thinly sliced

½ cup halved red seedless grapes

1 cup plain yogurt

4 cups arugula

pepper

Method

1 Toast the pecans in a skillet for a few minutes to bring out
   their flavor. When they are cool enough to handle, coarsely
   chop them.

2 Peel and chop the apples, then toss them in a bowl with the
   lemon juice to prevent them from discoloring.

3 Add the celery, grapes, and half the pecans to the apples
   and mix well. Stir in the yogurt and season with pepper, then
   gently toss together.

4 Divide the arugula among four serving plates and spoon over the
   salad mixture. Sprinkle the remaining nuts over the salad.

02

DRIED APRICOTS

Dried apricots are highly nutritious and contain high levels of carotenes and iron. They offer a range of benefits to women throughout menopause.

Apricots are a valuable source of the carotenoid group of compounds, one of which is lycopene. A high intake of lycopene can protect low-density lipoprotein (LDL) cholesterol from oxidation, which produces the damaging free radicals that are a major cause of the aging process. Another carotenoid, cryptoxanthin, helps to maintain bone health and density. Apricots also promote eye health because our bodies convert the carotenes they contain into vitamin A, which helps prevent the degeneration of our vision as we age. We get iron from them, too, which boosts our energy levels and brain function, helps prevent tiredness and hair loss, and protects the immune system. Dried apricots are ideal for dieters—their high fiber content means they are low on the glycemic index and, therefore, keep us feeling full. They are even fat-free.

- Contain carotenes that promote heart and bone health.
- Offer protection against some cancers and vision deterioration.
- High in fiber, which benefits the heart and blood and is an aid to weight control.

Practical tips:
Poach dried apricots in a little water until tender—this helps the carotenes and soluble fiber to be absorbed by the body. Consume in moderation if allergic to aspirin: dried apricots contain salicylate, a natural substance similar to the active ingredient in aspirin.

DID YOU KNOW?

Dried apricots and other dried fruit that are produced commercially are usually preserved with the aid of sulfites, which are thought to trigger asthma in susceptible people. However, organic dried fruit do not contain sulfites.

MAJOR NUTRIENTS PER 3 PIECES (1 oz.) SEMIDRIED APRICOTS

Calories	47
Total fat	Trace
Protein	1.2 g
Carbohydrate	10.8 g
Fiber	1.9 g
Vitamin C	Trace
Potassium	414 mg
Beta-carotene	163 mcg
Iron	1 mg

Exotic dried fruit compote

SERVES 4   (**W**) (**F**) (**B**) (**H**)

½ cup dried peaches
⅔ cup dried apricots
⅓ cup dried pineapple chunks
½ cup dried mango slices
1 cup unsweetened apple juice
¼ cup plain yogurt (optional)

Method

1 Put the dried fruit into a small saucepan with the apple juice. Slowly bring to a boil, then reduce the heat to low, cover, and simmer for 10 minutes.

2 Spoon into serving dishes and top each serving with a tablespoon of yogurt, if using. Serve immediately.

03

BLACKBERRIES

Blackberries are extremely rich in antioxidants, which offer protection from the aging process and the diseases most common in midlife. They are also a useful food for controlling weight.

At 5,905 units, blackberries rate higher on the latest oxygen radical absorbance capacity (ORAC) scale produced by the U.S. Nutrient Database than the more publicized blueberries, which score 4,669. The deep blue/purple color of the berries derives from several compounds, including ellagic acid and anthocyanins, which fight against heart disease, cancers, and the signs of aging. Blackberries also contain a good range of vitamins and minerals. Their vitamin C content works alongside the fruit's magnesium and calcium to help protect and strengthen bones, while the iron and zinc boost the immune system and help to regulate hormones. The high vitamin E content also helps to protect the heart, keep skin healthy, and may improve mood and concentration. As a high fiber, low-calorie food, blackberries are ideal for weight control.

- High on the ORAC antioxidant scale, which means blackberries help protect us from disease.
- Mineral content strengthens bones.
- Vitamin E protects the heart and skin.
- Low in calories and high in fiber, promoting weight control.

Practical tips:
Blackberries can be eaten raw, which means they retain their vitamin C content, but they are also good poached. Most of the antioxidant capacity remains after cooking.

DID YOU KNOW?

Women susceptible to asthma may be advised to avoid blackberries because they contain salicylate, which can cause an allergic reaction.

MAJOR NUTRIENTS PER ⅔ CUP (3½ OZ.) BLACKBERRIES

Calories	25
Total fat	Trace
Protein	0.9 g
Carbohydrate	5 g
Fiber	3.1 g
Vitamin C	15 mg
Potassium	160 mg
Calcium	41 mg
Iron	0.7 mg
Zinc	0.53 mg
Vitamin E	2.4 mg

Frozen berry yogurt

SERVES 4 (W) (B) (H) (M) (S)

1 cup raspberries
1 cup blackberries
1 cup strawberries
1 extra-large egg
¾ cup Greek-style yogurt
½ cup red wine
2¼ teaspoons powdered gelatin
fresh berries, to decorate

Method

1 Place the raspberries, blackberries, and strawberries in a food processor or blender and process until smooth. To remove the seeds, push the puree through a strainer into a bowl.

2 Break the egg and separate the yolk and white into different bowls. Stir the egg yolk and yogurt into the berry puree and set the egg white aside.

3 Pour the wine into a heatproof bowl and sprinkle the gelatin on the surface. Let stand for 5 minutes to soften, then set the bowl over a saucepan of simmering water until the gelatin has dissolved. Pour the mixture into the berry puree in a steady stream, beating continuously. Transfer the mixture to a freezer-proof container and freeze for 2 hours, or until slushy.

4 Beat the egg white in a spotlessly clean, grease-free bowl until very stiff. Remove the berry mixture from the freezer and fold in the egg white. Return to the freezer and freeze for an additional 2 hours, or until firm. To serve, scoop the berry yogurt ice into serving bowls and decorate with fresh berries of your choice.

04

BANANAS

Bananas have much to offer during menopause: they may help weight control, prevent diabetes and high blood pressure, and help to give a restful night's sleep.

Bananas are one of the few fruits that are high in starch, including a high level of resistant starch. Resistant starch is similar in quality to dietary fiber in that it literally resists being digested. As such, it helps keep the bowels regular, and it is also valuable in managing type 2 diabetes. The starches in banana help to prevent hunger, too, making this a useful food to include in weight-loss diets. Bananas are also a rich source of a prebiotic that helps the body to absorb calcium, which is essential for bone health. Among all the fruits, bananas contain one of the highest levels of the mineral potassium, which helps to regulate heart function as well as fluid balance and blood pressure. An average banana contains approximately one-quarter of our daily requirement for vitamin B6. This vitamin supports the function of the nervous system and prevents fatigue. Bananas also have a useful vitamin C content.

- Resistant starch helps manage type 2 diabetes and aids weight loss because it prevents hunger.
- Vitamin B6 alleviates fatigue and supports the nervous system.
- Very high potassium content helps control high blood pressure.

Practical tips:
Underripe bananas have the highest resistant starch content but ripe bananas are easier to digest because a lot of their starch has been converted to sugar. Bananas can be refrigerated and will not usually discolor, although the ripening process will be disrupted.

DID YOU KNOW?

Plantains are in the same family as bananas but are not so sweet and soft, hence they are usually served cooked. Although they have a similar nutritional profile to bananas, they contain considerably more carotene.

MAJOR NUTRIENTS PER AVERAGE-SIZE BANANA

Calories	89
Total fat	0.3 g
Protein	1 g
Carbohydrate	23 g
Fiber	2.6 g
Vitamin C	8.7 mg
Vitamin B6	0.37 mg
Folic acid	20 mcg
Iron	0.31 mg
Potassium	358 mg
Magnesium	27 mg

Orange and banana biscuits

MAKES 12   (B) (M)

sunflower oil, for oiling
¾ cup white all-purpose flour, plus
*   extra for dusting, and for rolling,*
*   if needed*
1⅔ cups whole-wheat flour
1½ tablespoons baking powder
½ teaspoon ground cinnamon
6 tablespoons unsalted butter,
*   diced and chilled*
¼ cup demerara sugar or other
*   raw sugar*
⅔ cup milk, plus extra
*   for brushing*
1 ripe banana, peeled and mashed
finely grated rind of 1 orange
1¼ cups fresh raspberries,
*   lightly mashed*

Method

1 Preheat the oven to 400°F. Lightly oil a baking sheet.
2 Mix together the flours, baking powder, and cinnamon in a large bowl, add the butter, and rub in with your fingertips until the mixture resembles bread crumbs. Stir in the sugar. Make a well in the middle of the dry ingredients and pour in the milk. Add the mashed banana and orange rind and mix to a soft dough. The dough will be quite wet.
3 Turn out the dough onto a lightly floured surface and, adding a little more flour, if needed, roll out to ¾ inch thick. Using a 2½-inch cookie cutter, cut out 12 biscuits, rerolling the dough trimmings where possible, and place them on the prepared baking sheet. Brush with milk and bake in the preheated oven for 10–12 minutes.
4 Remove from the oven and let cool slightly, then halve the biscuits and fill with the raspberries.

05

AVOCADOS

The avocado is packed with valuable nutrients for midlife health, including vitamin E and monounsaturated fats for our heart, and vitamin K for the bones.

Avocado is very high in fat, giving it a high calorie content. However, this fat is two-thirds monounsaturated, which is rich in oleic acid, a fatty acid that can lower the risk of breast cancer. It can also help to reduce LDL blood cholesterol levels, raise good high density lipoprotein (HDL) cholesterol, and lower the risk of heart disease. Avocados are high in vitamin E, too, which helps to minimize hot flashes and is important for heart health, good skin, and the immune system. They also have the immune-boosting antioxidant zinc, magnesium for healthy bones, nerves, energy, and heart function, and the antioxidant chemical glutathione, which protects against some cancers. Avocados are also surprisingly high in both vitamin C and potassium, and vitamin B6, which enables the body to balance hormones, soothes the nerves, and promotes energy.

- Vitamin E content can help with hot flashes, boost the immune system, keep skin healthy, and help prevent heart disease.
- Monounsaturated fat helps lower cholesterol.
- Magnesium and vitamin K keep bones healthy.

Practical tips:
Avocados are ready to eat when the flesh yields slightly when pressed with the thumb. The flesh naturally discolors within minutes once cut, but you can prevent this by brushing the cut surfaces with lemon juice or vinegar.

DID YOU KNOW?

The avocado is a native tree of Mexico. It is not related to the pear, although it is a fruit, not a vegetable.

MAJOR NUTRIENTS PER AVERAGE-SIZE AVOCADO

Calories	227
Total fat	21 g
Protein	2.6 g
Carbohydrate	12 g
Fiber	9.2 g
Vitamin C	12 mg
Magnesium	37 mg
Potassium	690 mg
Zinc	0.9 mg
Vitamin B6	0.39 mg
Vitamin E	3 mg
Vitamin K	28 ug

Chicken avocado salad

SERVES 4 (w) (h) (m) (s)

4½ cups mixed salad greens, such
    as beet leaves, frisée endive,
    and radicchio
3 cups shredded skinless,
    boneless, cooked chicken
2 satsumas, separated into
    segments
2 celery stalks, thinly sliced
½ red onion, halved and
    thinly sliced
2 tablespoons finely snipped
    fresh chives
2 avocados
toasted sunflower seeds, to garnish
whole-wheat pita bread, to serve

Dressing
½ cup extra virgin olive oil
3 tablespoons white wine vinegar
½ teaspoon Dijon mustard

Method

1 To make the dressing, put all the ingredients into a small screw-top
  jar and shake until well blended.
2 Put the salad greens into a bowl, add about one-third of the
  dressing, and lightly toss. Add the chicken, satsumas, celery,
  onion, chives, and the remaining dressing and toss again.
3 Cut the avocados in half and remove the pit, then peel away the
  skin. Cut the flesh into thin slices, add to the other ingredients,
  and gently toss together, making sure the avocado slices are
  completely coated with dressing so they don't discolor.
4 Arrange on serving plates, sprinkle sunflower seeds over the
  top, and serve immediately with whole-wheat pita bread.

06 CHERRIES

Cherries are an excellent source of several antioxidants, which supercharge our health in midlife and help protect us against disease. They also contribute to the smooth running of our digestive systems.

The major nutritional benefit of this sweet glossy fruit is that cherries are rich in plant compounds that can slow down the signs of aging and help to beat disease. At 3,747, they have a high ORAC rating and are particularly rich in cyanidin, which is anti-inflammatory and can help to relieve the symptoms of arthritis, headaches, and gout, as well as offering protection against heart disease and cancer. Cherries also contain quercetin, a flavonoid, and carotenes, both of which have anticancer and heart-protecting qualities. Black and deep red cherries contain more of these important chemicals than white or yellow varieties. Cherries have a laxative effect, which helps cleanse the digestive system. Their high potassium content helps the kidneys eliminate excess fluid. Low on the glycemic index, cherries aid weight loss, while their soluble fiber content helps control LDL blood cholesterol levels.

- One of the best fruit sources of antioxidants, which help us beat the signs and diseases of aging.
- Cyanidin content alleviates arthritis and inflammatory diseases.
- A useful digestive and dieting aid.

Practical tips:
Store cherries in the refrigerator to keep fresh and maintain their vitamin C content. Glossy skin is a sign of freshness. Darker cherries contain much higher levels of antioxidants.

DID YOU KNOW?
Sour cherries, which are more tart than sweet cherries, tend to contain slightly higher levels of vitamins and minerals. They need to be cooked before eating, however, which destroys their vitamin C content.

MAJOR NUTRIENTS PER ⅔ CUP (3½ OZ.) FRESH SWEET CHERRIES

Calories	63
Total fat	Trace
Protein	1g
Carbohydrate	16 g
Fiber	2.1 g
Vitamin C	7 mg
Potassium	222 mg

Cherry yogurt sundae

SERVES 2   (**W**) (**B**) (**H**) (**M**)

1 cup hulled strawberries

1–2 teaspoons honey, to taste

1 teaspoon vanilla bean paste or vanilla extract

1 cup plain yogurt with active cultures

1 cup fresh pitted and halved cherries

⅓ cup coarsely chopped hazelnuts

Method

1 Put the strawberries in a food processor or blender and process until smooth. Transfer to a bowl, then stir in the honey with the vanilla bean paste. Lightly stir the strawberry-and-vanilla sauce into the yogurt.

2 Divide the cherries between two serving dishes before topping with the strawberry yogurt mixture. Sprinkle the hazelnuts over them before serving.

07

CRANBERRIES

These small red berries pack a powerful punch of plant chemicals that can help improve menopausal health. They are also a good source of important vitamins.

Cranberries contain at least five categories of health-promoting chemicals: phenols, flavonoids, terpenes, anthocyanins, and proanthocyanins. All of these nutritional gems have antioxidant, antiaging, and anti-inflammatory properties, which means cranberries help to protect us against a range of cancers, including breast, stomach, and colon cancers. They are also known to benefit heart health, mainly because of their pterostilbene content, a compound that helps inhibit oxidation of LDL cholesterol and keeps the arteries healthy. Their anthocyanin content helps maintain good vision and eye health. Cranberries protect against urinary tract infections, which some women are more prone to in later life. They are a good source of vitamin C, which boosts brain function and mood, and vitamin E, which helps improve skin condition and may help to reduce hot flashes, and fiber.

- Offer protection against cancers and the diseases of aging.
- Keep arteries supple and improve the balance of "good" to "bad" fats circulating in our blood.
- High in vitamin E, which improves skin quality and can reduce hot flashes.

Practical tips:
Fresh, whole cranberries offer even more health benefits than dried ones or cranberry juice. Choose berries with smooth, bright skin; any wrinkling means that the fruit is past its best.

DID YOU KNOW?

People who take warfarin anticoagulants should avoid eating cranberries or drinking cranberry juice; the berry can raise the level of this drug in the blood with dangerous consequences.

MAJOR NUTRIENTS PER 1 CUP (3½ OZ.) RAW CRANBERRIES

Calories	46
Total fat	Trace
Protein	0.4 g
Carbohydrate	12.2 g
Fiber	4.6 g
Vitamin C	13 g
Vitamin E	1.2 mg

Cranberry and orange smoothie

SERVES 1–2 Ⓦ Ⓑ Ⓗ

1 orange
½ cup cranberries
1 banana
½ cup plain yogurt
fine shreds of orange zest,
*   to decorate*

Method

1 Peel the orange, leaving some of the white pith.

2 Put the orange and cranberries in a food processor or blender and process until smooth. Add the peeled banana and yogurt, then blend together.

3 Pour into glasses, sprinkle shreds of orange zest over the top, and serve.

08

FIGS

The range of minerals and vitamins figs offer can help maintain energy levels and alleviate other menopausal symptoms, such as fluid retention and insomnia.

MAJOR NUTRIENTS PER 2 SMALL (2¾ oz.) FRESH FIGS

Calories	59
Total fat	Trace
Protein	0.5 g
Carbohydrate	15 g
Fiber	2.3 g
Potassium	186 mg
Calcium	28 mg
Magnesium	11 mg
Iron	0.3 mg

MAJOR NUTRIENTS PER 3 (1 oz.) DRIED FIGS

Calories	62
Total fat	Trace
Protein	0.8 g
Carbohydrate	16 g
Fiber	2.5 g
Potassium	170 mg
Calcium	41 mg
Magnesium	17 mg
Iron	0.5 mg

Figs are most often purchased in their dried or semidried form because the fresh fruit has a short shelf life and damages easily. Both fresh and dried figs are nutritious, containing a range of vitamins and minerals that can reduce menopausal symptoms. They also have a good (fresh) to excellent (dried) fiber content. Much of this fiber is soluble, which helps lower blood LDL cholesterol and, therefore, protect against heart disease. The effect is enhanced by the fig's natural plant sterols. The high fiber content of this fruit is what gives figs their reputation as a cure for constipation or bowel irregularity. Dried figs are a concentrated source of iron, and eating them regularly can help memory and concentration and boost energy levels. Eat a handful before going to bed and you will improve the quality of your sleep, too.

• Contain soluble fiber and sterols, which lower blood cholesterol.
• Potassium content helps prevent fluid retention.
• Dried figs are a good source of iron, which keeps the blood healthy and gives us energy.
• Dried figs are a good source of calcium, needed for strong bones.

Practical tips:
Fresh figs should be eaten the day they are bought because they spoil quickly. Keep them in the refrigerator until ready to eat. You can eat the skins of most varieties, but wipe gently with a damp cloth to clean.

Fig and watermelon salad

SERVES 4   (**W**) (**F**) (**H**) (**S**)

1 watermelon (about 3¼ pounds)
¾ cup seedless red grapes
4 figs

Dressing
grated rind of 1 lime
grated rind and juice of 1 orange
1 teaspoon maple syrup
2 teaspoons honey

Method

1 Cut the watermelon into quarters and scoop out and discard the seeds. Cut the flesh away from the rind, then chop the flesh into 1-inch cubes. Place the watermelon cubes in a bowl with the grapes. Cut each fig lengthwise into 8 wedges and add to the bowl.

2 To make the dressing, mix the lime rind with the orange rind and juice, maple syrup, and honey in a small saucepan. Bring to a boil over low heat. Pour the mixture over the fruit and stir. Let cool. Stir again, cover, and chill in the refrigerator for at least 1 hour, stirring occasionally.

3 Divide the fruit salad equally among four serving bowls and serve.

09 GRAPEFRUIT

Grapefruit is an excellent source of vitamin C and carotenes. These valuable nutrients work hard to boost the immune system and help protect us from heart disease and cancers.

Just one fruit contains more than our daily requirement of vitamin C, a powerful antioxidant that can help minimize the progress of arthritis and help to prevent heart and arterial disease; conditions that become more common after menopause. Vitamin C is also linked with improved mood, memory, and concentration. The bioflavonoids in grapefruit appear to enhance the effects of vitamin C, while naringenin, a plant chemical, can help to lower LDL cholesterol. Pink-fleshed grapefruit is a good source of lycopene, the carotene pigment that helps fight cancer and protect our cells from the signs of aging. Grapefruit pulp (the flesh plus pith) contains glucarates, the compounds that may help prevent breast cancer. What's more, grapefruits are low on the glycemic index, high in the soluble fiber pectin, which helps control hunger, and low in calories, making them ideal for weight management.

- High in vitamin C, which helps minimize the risk of diseases of later life and to boost mood and memory.
- Plant compounds protect against heart disease and cancers.
- Ideal fruit for dieters.

Practical tips:
The white pith is high in beneficial compounds. A completely ripe grapefruit contains the maximum amount of antioxidants. Choose a fruit that feels heavy in the hand, because this is a sign it is juicy.

DID YOU KNOW?
Because grapefruit juice can alter the effect of certain medicines, including ones that lower blood pressure, anyone on medication should first check with their doctor that it is safe to consume the fruit or the juice.

MAJOR NUTRIENTS PER HALF AVERAGE-SIZE PINK GRAPEFRUIT

Calories	30
Total fat	Trace
Protein	0.5 g
Carbohydrate	7.5 g
Fiber	1.1 g
Vitamin C	37 mg
Folic acid	9 mcg
Potassium	127 mg
Calcium	15 mg
Beta-carotene	770 mcg

Grapefruit cups

SERVES 4 (**W**) (**B**) (**S**)

2 red or pink grapefruit,
about 1 pound each
2 tablespoons demerara sugar
or other raw sugar
2 ripe passion fruit or
2 tablespoons orange flower
water (optional)

Method

1 Preheat the broiler to medium and line the broiler rack with
aluminum foil. Cut the grapefruits in half and, using a grapefruit knife
or small, sharp-pointed knife, carefully loosen the segments and
remove the middle section of pith. Carefully cut under the segments
to make them easier to remove later.

2 Put the grapefruits on the foil-lined rack and sprinkle with the sugar.
Cook under the broiler for 5 minutes, or until the sugar has melted.

3 If using passion fruit, cut in half, scoop out the seeds and flesh, and
spoon them over the cooked grapefruit. Alternatively, pour the
orange flower water over the grapefruit. Serve half a grapefruit per
person while still hot.

10 BLUEBERRIES

These deep purple berries are becoming increasingly popular as we begin to understand the many health benefits they have to offer.

As one of the highest fruits on the ORAC scale, blueberries are supremely rich in antioxidants. Antioxidants are believed to help protect us from the diseases of aging and the general degeneration that aging produces. One important antioxidant contained in the berries is the compound pterostilbene, which seems to be as effective as commercial medicines in lowering cholesterol, and can also help protect us from type 2 diabetes, which may occur in midlife. Another is the anthocyanin group, which can help prevent heart disease and memory loss. The polyphenols in blueberries may even break down fat cells and prevent new ones from forming, which is excellent news for dieters. Blueberries are also a good source of dietary fiber, so they can ease digestive problems, and contain good amounts of vitamin C.

- Can act as an aid in dieting and as a digestive aid.
- Contain the cholesterol-lowering compound pterostilbene.
- Can help prevent many of the major diseases, including coronary heart disease and diabetes.
- Can improve memory and brain function.

Practical tips:
Blueberries are sweet enough to eat as they are, which gives us the maximum level of vitamin C. Try adding a handful of blueberries to your breakfast cereal or yogurt. Berries freeze well and lose almost none of their nutrients in this way.

DID YOU KNOW?

Wild blueberries—sometimes called "huckleberries"— are higher in antioxidant compounds than cultivated blueberries, but all types are a rich source of plant chemicals.

MAJOR NUTRIENTS PER ⅓ CUP (1¾ OZ.) BLUEBERRIES

Calories	29
Total fat	Trace
Protein	0.4 g
Carbohydrate	7.2 g
Fiber	1.2 g
Vitamin C	5 mg
Potassium	39 mg
Iron	0.7 mg
Vitamin E	2.4 mg

Honey and blueberry crunch bars

MAKES 10–12   (M) (S)

sunflower oil, for oiling
⅔ cup all-purpose flour
1 teaspoon baking powder
½ cup quinoa flakes
3⅔ cups puffed rice
½ cup slivered almonds
1½ cups blueberries
1 stick butter
½ cup honey
1 egg, beaten

Method

1 Preheat the oven to 350°F. Oil an 11 x 7-inch baking pan and line the bottom with nonstick parchment paper.

2 Mix together the flour, baking powder, quinoa, puffed rice, almonds, and blueberries. Place the butter and honey in a saucepan over low heat until just melted, then stir evenly into the dry ingredients with the egg.

3 Spread the mixture into the prepared pan, smoothing with a rubber spatula. Bake in the preheated oven for 25–30 minutes, until golden brown and firm.

4 Let cool in the pan for 15 minutes, then cut into 10–12 bars. Transfer to a wire rack to continue cooling.

11

KIWI

The bright green flesh of the kiwi contains many potent plant chemicals that offer a valuable contribution to health and well-being, while the black seeds boost the fruit's important fiber content.

Kiwi is one of the few fruits to have green flesh when it is ripe. Its color comes from chlorophyll, the plant chemical that is necessary for plant photosynthesis. In our bodies, chlorophyll converts to cancer-fighting compounds similar to those found in green tea. When kiwi juice is consumed with nitrate-containing foods, such as bacon and cured meats, it blocks the formation of nitrosamine, which is linked with breast and other cancers. Kiwis have a high vitamin C content, too, and regular consumption of this fruit is recognized as an important aid to lowering the risk of heart and arterial disease. Kiwi is high in fiber, which promotes digestive health and bowel regularity, while the high potassium content can help reduce blood pressure. It contains good levels of folic acid for heart health, calcium for bone strength, vitamin E for our skin, and lutein and zeaxanthin to protect our eyes.

- Chlorophyll helps protect against cancers.
- Vitamin C offers protection against heart disease.
- High in fiber, necessary for digestive health.
- Good source of vitamin E, which gives us younger looking skin.

Practical tips:
Don't cut kiwi until you are ready to eat it, because it starts to lose vitamin C immediately. It contains actinidin, a meat tenderizer, so kiwi juice is excellent for marinating meat before cooking.

DID YOU KNOW?

The actinidin in raw kiwi is not only a tenderizer but also prevents gelatin from setting and will cause milk and cream to curdle. For this reason, the fruit/juice cannot be used in gelatins or milk desserts.

MAJOR NUTRIENTS PER AVERAGE-SIZE KIWI

Calories	42
Total fat	0.3 g
Protein	0.8 g
Carbohydrate	10 g
Fiber	2.1 g
Vitamin C	64 mg
Vitamin E	1 mg
Folic acid	17 mcg
Potassium	215 mg
Calcium	23 mg
Lutein/Zeaxanthin	84 mg

Kiwi juice

SERVES 1–2 (W) (B) (H) (S)

1 kiwi
1 apple
¾ cup seedless white grapes

Method

1 Put all the ingredients in a food processor or blender and process until smooth.
2 Pour into glasses and serve just as it is, or pour over ice.

12 GRAPES

Grapes contain several polyphenol antioxidants. These plant compounds can protect us from cardiovascular disease, breast cancer, and Alzheimer's disease.

Red and purple grapes are the ones to go for when it comes to health protection in midlife. The skins of darker grapes contain resveratrol, a compound that is a strong antioxidant, helping to beat heart disease and delay the signs of aging. It can improve blood flow to the brain by 30 percent and is believed to help prevent Alzheimer's disease. Pterostilbene, a derivative of resveratrol, has been found in laboratory tests to destroy breast cancer cells. It also has antidiabetic properties because it helps to regulate blood glucose levels. The dark grape skins—and seeds— contain the flavonoid quercetin, which is not only antioxidant but appears to boost energy levels, and anthocyanin, another type of powerful disease-beating compound. The skin also contains saponins, which can help prevent the absorption of cholesterol, and tannins, which protect against disease.

- Rich source of a variety of antioxidants, offering cancer prevention and ensuring a healthy cardiovascular system.
- Resveratrol helps brain function and may prevent Alzheimer's.
- Pterostilbene destroys breast cancer cells and is antidiabetic.
- Quercetin can improve your blood cholesterol profile.

Practical tips:
Store grapes in the refrigerator. Unless they are organic, wash before use in case they were sprayed with pesticides. Don't cut them until the last minute to prevent oxidation of the cut side.

DID YOU KNOW?
When several best-selling fruit juices were tested under scientific conditions for their antioxidant capacity, purple (Concord) grape juice came out top, while white grape juice had the lowest score.

MAJOR NUTRIENTS PER ⅔ CUP (3½ OZ.) GRAPES

Calories	70
Total fat	Trace
Protein	0.7 g
Carbohydrate	18 g
Fiber	0.9 g
Vitamin C	10.8 mg
Potassium	191 mg

Grape and strawberry smoothie

SERVES 1 (W)(B)(H)(S)

8 ounces strawberries, hulled
¾ cup seedless red grapes
½ cup red grape or cranberry juice, chilled
small bunch of red grapes, to decorate

Method

1 Halve the strawberries, if large, and peel the grapes if you like, then place both fruits into a food processor or blender. Add the juice and process until smooth.

2 Pour into a glass, add the grapes to decorate, and serve immediately.

13

LEMONS

While few of us would eat a lemon whole, it is well worth including these sharp, tangy fruits in your diet. Lemons are an excellent source of vitamin C, and contain several beneficial plant compounds.

Limonene, found mainly in lemon peel, is an antioxidant oil that appears to help prevent breast cancer and may help to lower LDL blood cholesterol. Rutin, also found mainly in the peel and pith of the fruit, has been found to strengthen veins and may help prevent varicose veins and thread veins, two common problems around menopause. The citric acid in the juice helps slow down the rate at which carbohydrates are absorbed in the digestive system, meaning we feel fuller for longer. The high pectin content of the fruit has a similar effect. In addition, the vitamin C and compounds in lemon produce an amino acid called carnitine, which helps the body to burn fat more quickly and speeds up the metabolic rate, making this a useful fruit for dieters.

- Limonene fights breast cancer and lowers LDL cholesterol.
- Rutin helps strengthen veins and prevent fluid retention.
- Citric acid and pectin helps slow carbohydrate absorption and prevent hunger.
- Encourage the body to burn fat.

DID YOU KNOW?

Very ripe lemons contain almost double the level of antioxidant compounds than paler, underripe fruits. Storing at room temperature can help to ripen the fruit and achieve this increase.

MAJOR NUTRIENTS PER AVERAGE-SIZE LEMON

Calories	17
Total fat	Trace
Protein	0.6 g
Carbohydrate	5.4 g
Fiber	1.6 g
Vitamin C	31 mg
Potassium	80 mg

Practical tips:

To get the maximum juice from a lemon, warm it for 10 seconds in the microwave before cutting and squeezing. Always buy unwaxed organic lemons if using the peel. Try lemon juice instead of vinegar in salad dressings, and use as a tenderizer in meat marinades.

Chicken in lemon and garlic

SERVES 6–8   (**W**) (**F**) (**H**)

4 large skinless, boneless
   chicken breasts
⅓ cup extra virgin olive oil
1 onion, finely chopped
6 garlic cloves, finely chopped
grated rind of 1 lemon, finely pared
   zest of 1 lemon, and juice
   of both lemons
¼ cup chopped fresh
   flat-leaf parsley
salt and pepper
lemon wedges and crusty bread,
   to serve

Method

1 Using a sharp knife, slice the chicken breasts widthwise into very thin slices. Heat the olive oil in a large, heavy skillet, add the onion, and sauté for 5 minutes, or until softened but not browned. Add the garlic and sauté for an addtional 30 seconds.

2 Add the sliced chicken to the skillet and cook gently for 5–10 minutes, stirring from time to time, until all the ingredients are lightly browned and the chicken is tender.

3 Add the grated lemon rind and the lemon juice and let it simmer. At the same time, deglaze the skillet by scraping and stirring all the sediment on the bottom of the skillet into the juices with a wooden spoon. Remove the skillet from the heat, stir in the parsley, and season with salt and pepper.

4 Transfer to a serving dish and sprinkle the lemon zest over the top. Serve with lemon wedges for squeezing over the chicken, accompanied by crusty bread for mopping up the lemon and garlic juices.

14 MANGOES

Sweet, juicy mangoes contain more vitamins and carotenes than most other fruit. They are also high in fiber and low on the glycemic index.

Mangoes are rich in the antioxidant beta-carotene, which helps protect us against breast and other cancers and heart disease. Mangoes are also rich in vitamin C, a powerful antioxidant that can help lift the low mood that commonly accompanies menopause. Meanwhile, the dietary fiber content, which includes the soluble fiber pectin, works to lower blood cholesterol and provide support to the digestive system. Mangoes are also a good source of potassium, which helps moderate high blood pressure. The significant vitamin E content maintains healthy, smooth skin and may protect against hot flashes. Because they have a medium–low rating on the glycemic index, mangoes are a good fruit for dieters. They also contain enzymes similar to those found in papaya, which soothe digestive discomfort.

- Contain carotenes and many other antioxidant compounds that offer protection against heart disease and cancers.
- Valuable source of vitamin C, a powerful mood booster.
- Pectin helps reduce LDL blood cholesterol.
- Good source of potassium, which regulates blood pressure.

Practical tips:
The carotenes in mangoes are better absorbed if you eat them with a little fat—for example, as part of a salad dressed with oil. Eat with red meat or other rich sources of iron and the vitamin C in mangoes will help your body to absorb the iron.

DID YOU KNOW?
Mangoes are one of the most popular fruits in the world. Originating in Asia, they have been cultivated for over 4,000 years.

MAJOR NUTRIENTS PER HALF AVERAGE-SIZE MANGO

Calories	101
Total fat	0.6 g
Protein	1.4 g
Carbohydrate	25 g
Fiber	2.7 g
Vitamin C	61 mg
Vitamin E	1.5 mg
Folic acid	72 mcg
Beta-carotene	1,075 mcg
Potassium	282 mg
Magnesium	12 mg

Shrimp and mango salad

SERVES 4   (w) (s)

2 mangoes
8 ounces cooked, peeled shrimp
4 cooked, unpeeled shrimp,
    to garnish
salad greens, to serve

Dressing

juice from the mangoes
⅓ cup plain yogurt
2 tablespoons mayonnaise
1 tablespoon lemon juice
salt and pepper

Method

1   Cutting close to the pit, cut a large segment from one side of each mango, then cut another segment from the opposite side. Without breaking the skin, cut the flesh in the segments into squares, then push the skin inside out to expose the cubes and cut them away from the skin. Use a sharp knife to peel the remaining center section of the mango and cut the flesh away from the pit into cubes. Reserve any juice in a bowl and put the mango flesh in a separate bowl. Add the peeled shrimp to the mango flesh.

2   To make the dressing, mix together the mango juice and yogurt, mayonnaise, lemon juice, and salt and pepper until well blended.

3   Arrange the salad greens on a serving dish and add the mango flesh and peeled shrimp. Pour the dressing over the salad and serve immediately, garnished with the unpeeled shrimp.

15

RHUBARB

Rhubarb appears to be of real help in minimizing many of the symptoms of menopause. It is both a laxative and a diuretic and may help prevent insulin resistance, diabetes, and weight gain.

Researchers in Germany have found that extract of rhubarb, taken in pill form, significantly reduces the frequency and severity of hot flashes in perimenopausal women. Rhubarb has also been found to reduce other menopausal symptoms, including insomnia and poor-quality sleep, mood changes, and vaginal dryness—although research has yet to discover exactly how it works. It has other health benefits, too. It seems to "mop up" LDL cholesterol in the body and reduce the risk of arterial disease and stroke. Its high potassium and low sodium content can help reduce high blood pressure, and its low calorie and fat content and good fiber content means it is a useful food for weight gain prevention. As a source of vitamin K, it offers protection against type 2 diabetes. This vitamin, working in conjunction with the calcium in rhubarb, is also vital for bone maintenance.

DID YOU KNOW?

The leaf of the rhubarb plant is toxic and high in oxalic acid, which prevents mineral absorption in the body. The stalks are completely safe, but the part of the stalk directly below the leaf—often greener than the rest of the stalk—is best avoided.

- Shown to reduce the severity and frequency of hot flashes and other common perimenopausal symptoms.
- Vitamin K helps prevent insulin resistance and diabetes.
- Helps lower cholesterol and blood pressure.

MAJOR NUTRIENTS PER 2 STALKS (3½ oz.) RHUBARB

Calories	21
Total fat	0.2 g
Protein	0.9 g
Carbohydrate	4.5 g
Fiber	1.8 g
Vitamin C	8 mg
Vitamin K	29 mcg
Potassium	288 mg
Calcium	86 mg

Practical tips:

Rhubarb is too sour and tough to eat raw—poach or bake it in a small amount of water. Adding cinnamon while cooking means you will need to add less sugar or honey to make it palatable.

Rhubarb strudel

SERVES 6 (H) (M)

1½ pounds rhubarb, trimmed and
    cut into 1¼-inch chunks
¼ cup firmly packed dark
    brown sugar
grated rind and segments
    of 1 orange
½ cup fresh white bread crumbs
½ cup slivered almonds
¼ teaspoon grated nutmeg
6 sheets of phyllo pastry
2½ tablespoons butter, melted
confectioners' sugar, for dusting
crème fraîche or Greek-style
    yogurt, to serve (optional)

Method

1 Preheat the oven to 400°F.
2 Place the rhubarb in a roasting pan and toss with half of the sugar.
   Roast for 20 minutes, tossing the rhubarb again after 10 minutes.
   Drain the rhubarb, reserving the liquid. Let cool slightly.
3 Place the grated orange rind and orange segments in a bowl with
   the rhubarb, bread crumbs, slivered almonds, and grated nutmeg
   and gently mix together.
4 Place one sheet of phyllo onto the work surface and brush with
   melted butter. Place another sheet on top and brush this with butter,
   too. Repeat with the remaining sheets of phyllo. Spoon the rhubarb
   mixture down the center of the phyllo pastry and sprinkle with the
   remaining sugar. Fold in the ends of the pastry, then roll the longest
   side over to make a long strudel shape. Brush the strudel with the
   remaining melted butter.
5 Reduce the oven temperature to 375°F. Bake the strudel for
   30 minutes, until golden. Remove from the oven and dust lightly
   with confectioners' sugar.
6 Serve hot with crème fraîche or yogurt, if using, and the reserved
   rhubarb juices.

16 MELONS

The juicy flesh of the melon is rich in vitamin C. It is an excellent food for rehydration and weight control, and it is also a useful source of potassium, which helps prevent fluid retention.

All melons have a high water content, which means that they are also low in calories and great for rehydration. Melons with orange flesh, such as cantaloupes, are high in carotenes, which have several health benefits, including lowering the risk of heart and arterial disease and helping to prevent breast and other cancers. Watermelon, with its deep red flesh, is high in lycopene, another cancer-preventive compound. It also contains citrulline, an amino acid that aids blood flow to the muscles and may help to make exercising easier as we age. Melons are also a good source of soluble fiber, which helps lower blood cholesterol and maintain healthy arteries. The seeds of the fruit can be dried and eaten, too. They are high in magnesium, which supports healthy heart and bones and is a useful tool in beating insomnia.

- Excellent fruit for exercisers and dieters.
- Beta-carotene content helps prevent the diseases of aging.
- High potassium content helps prevent fluid retention and reduce high blood pressure.
- Fiber benefits arteries and can help lower LDL blood cholesterol.

Practical tips:
Try to buy whole melons instead of packaged cut slices. Store them at room temperature and, if you like to eat them cold, chill for an hour before cutting.

DID YOU KNOW?

The riper a melon, the more antioxidant compounds it contains. You can tell when a melon is ripe because it will give a little when pressed with the thumb and gives off its distinctive aromas.

MAJOR NUTRIENTS PER ⅔ CUP DICED (3½ OZ.) CANTALOUPE MELON, EXCLUDING SKIN

Calories	34
Total fat	Trace
Protein	0.8 g
Carbohydrate	8 g
Fiber	1 g
Vitamin C	37 mg
Potassium	267 mg
Beta-carotene	2,020 mcg

Melon sorbet

SERVES 4 (W)(H)(S)

1 ripe melon, peeled, seeded,
and cut into chunks
juice of 2 limes
¼ cup unrefined sugar
1 egg white, lightly beaten
fresh strawberries or raspberries,
to serve

Method

1 Put the melon and lime juice into a food processor or blender and process until smooth. Pour into a large measuring cup and make up to 2½ cups with cold water.
2 Pour into a bowl and stir in the sugar. Beat in the egg white.
3 Transfer to a freezer-proof container and freeze for 6 hours.
4 Serve with strawberries.

17

NECTARINES

The nectarine is a cousin of the peach but has smooth skin, juicier flesh, and a higher vitamin C content. They are rich in antioxidants, which offer a variety of benefits during and after menopause.

An average nectarine contains your whole day's requirement of vitamin C. Sufficient intake of this vitamin is vital during menopause because it helps counteract depression, low mood, and problems with memory and concentration. The fruit also contains two other antioxidants that work synergistically with vitamin C—carotenes, which convert to vitamin A in the body and help improve memory, skin condition, and protect against cancer, and vitamin E, which helps combat dry skin, vaginal dryness, and protects against heart disease. Nectarines are also high in pectin, the soluble fiber that can help to improve your blood lipids profile and lower LDL cholesterol. The skin of the nectarine is high in insoluble fiber, which means it helps prevent constipation, and the fruit is also rich in potassium, which acts as a diuretic, minimizing fluid retention and helping to improve high blood pressure.

- Vitamin C helps to boost mood and memory.
- Vitamins A and E improve skin and protect against disease.
- Rich in fibers, including pectin that keeps blood healthy, and insoluble fiber that prevents constipation.

Practical tips:
Nectarines are one of the very best fruits to eat raw, but they need to be perfectly ripe to have their full, juicy flavor. A nectarine is ripe when it gives under gentle pressure and has a sweet fragrance.

DID YOU KNOW?
Nectarines are an ancient fruit and are named after the Greek god Nekter. This is why the juice of the fruit is sometimes called the "drink of the gods."

MAJOR NUTRIENTS PER AVERAGE-SIZE NECTARINE

Calories	65
Total fat	0.4 g
Protein	1.5 g
Carbohydrate	15 g
Fiber	2.4 g
Vitamin C	55 mg
Vitamin E	1 mg
Potassium	285 mg

Nectarine, feta, and arugula salad

SERVES 4   (**W**) (**H**) (**B**)

6 cups arugula (about 3½ ounces)

4 nectarines, halved, pitted, and
cut into thin wedges

2 tablespoons pumpkin seeds,
toasted

1 cup crumbled, drained feta
cheese

Dressing

3 tablespoons olive oil

juice of ½ lemon

½ teaspoon honey

½ teaspoon whole-grain mustard

Method

1 To make the dressing, mix together the olive oil, lemon juice, honey, and mustard in a bowl.

2 Place the arugula, nectarine wedges, pumpkin seeds, and feta cheese in a serving bowl.

3 Pour the dressing over the salad and gently toss to coat. Serve immediately.

18 PLUMS

Plums are full of phenolic compounds—antioxidants that protect the brain as well as the heart. Low on the glycemic index, they are excellent for dieters.

In general, the deeper/brighter the color of the plum's skin and flesh, the more antioxidant compounds the fruit will contain. Plums are an excellent source of the phenolic compounds neochlorogenic and chlorogenic acid, which neutralize the free radicals produced in our bodies during everyday living and as we age. Research has shown that these compounds are particularly effective at keeping the brain and blood cholesterol healthy. Red and purple plums are also rich in anthocyanins, which help prevent heart disease, breast and other cancers, and varicose veins. Research suggests that a component of plum—so far unidentified—helps the body absorb iron. This is useful because iron is often poorly absorbed and a deficiency can lead to tiredness and lack of energy and stamina.

- Rich in phenolic compounds that nourish the brain and have strong antioxidant action.
- Useful for helping to control weight.
- Good source of carotenes, which offer protection from cancer and support eye health.
- Studies show eating plums helps us absorb iron.

Practical tips:
Let plums ripen completely at room temperature before eating. Ripe plums contain more of the beneficial antioxidants than unripe ones. To cook, poach plums in a small amount of water over low heat; eat the juice, because some of the nutrients will leach into it.

DID YOU KNOW?

There are over 2,000 varieties of plum. Damsons are a small, purple-black type that are inedible raw, but once cooked are one of the richest antioxidant sources of all the varieties.

MAJOR NUTRIENTS PER AVERAGE-SIZE PLUM

Calories	30
Total fat	Trace
Protein	0.5 g
Carbohydrate	7.5 g
Fiber	0.9 g
Vitamin C	6.3 mg
Beta-carotene	125 mcg
Lutein/Zeaxanthin	48 mcg
Potassium	104 mg
Iron	0.4 mg

Plum shake

SERVES 2 (W) (F) (H)

4 ripe plums
1 cup water
1 tablespoon sugar
4 scoops plain frozen yogurt
sliced plums and 2 crumbled
*   almond biscotti, to decorate*

Method

1 Put the plums, water, and sugar into a small saucepan. Cover tightly and simmer for about 15 minutes, until the plums have split and are soft. Let cool.

2 Strain off the liquid into a food processor or blender and add the frozen yogurt. Process until smooth and frothy.

3 Pour into glasses and decorate each of the rims with a slice of plum. Sprinkle with the crumbled biscotti and serve.

19

OLIVES

Olives are one of our richest sources of monounsaturated fats. They also contain a range of nutrients that have anti-inflammatory effects and other benefits.

One of the oldest known foods in the world, olives are grown mainly for their high oil content. The oil is high in monounsaturated fats, 75 percent of which is a particularly useful form of monounsaturate called oleic acid. This fatty acid is known to lower harmful cholesterol and to help prevent cardiovascular disease. The fruit is also high in vitamin E, a powerful antioxidant vitamin that is of special benefit during and after menopause because it helps to keep the skin looking and feeling smooth. The vitamin can help reduce the frequency and severity of hot flashes, too. The anti-inflammatory actions of the monounsaturated fats, vitamin E, and various phenols and flavonoids in combination may help control osteoarthritis and rheumatoid arthritis and prevent cancer. This tasty fruit is also high in lutein and zeaxanthin, which are needed to keep the eyes healthy as we grow older.

- Oleic acid content lowers cholesterol and helps prevent cardiovascular disease.
- Vitamin E keeps skin smooth and can help control hot flashes.
- Antioxidants provide protection from arthritis and cancers.

Practical tips:
You can slice olives and add them to all kinds of salads, pizzas, and stews, or eat them as a snack. Try to buy ones that have been preserved without the addition of brine, especially if you have high blood pressure, because the sodium content will be lower.

DID YOU KNOW?

Olives cannot be eaten straight off the tree as you would a cherry. They are too bitter to eat fresh and need to be processed.

MAJOR NUTRIENTS PER 6 (1½ oz.) OLIVES

Calories	46
Total fat	4.3 g
Protein	0.3 g
Carbohydrate	2.5 g
Fiber	1.3 g
Vitamin E	0.7 mg
Iron	1.3 mg
Sodium	294 mg
Calcium	35 mg
Lutein/Zeaxanthin	20 mcg

Crushed olive potatoes

SERVES 4 (H) (M) (S)

*12 new potatoes, unpeeled,
    and halved if large*
*¾ cup pitted ripe black or
    green olives*
1½ tablespoons extra virgin olive oil
broiled fish and a salad, to serve

Method

1 Cook the potatoes in a saucepan of boiling water until tender,
    then drain.

2 Place the olives and olive oil in a small food processor or blender
    and process until broken up but still chunky.

3 Using a fork, add the olive mixture to the potatoes, lightly crushing
    the potatoes while stirring it in.

4 Serve hot as an accompaniment to broiled fish and salad.

20 PRUNES

Prunes are the dried fruit of certain types of plum, and are high in sugars and acids. They have several compounds of particular benefit for women during menopause.

Prunes have a total ORAC score of 8,059, one of the highest scores of all fruit. This is partly because, as they are dried, their water content is low and their nutrient content high. Their antioxidant compounds include phenols, which keep the brain and cholesterol healthy; hydroxycinnamic acids, which reduce our risk of cancer; and carotenes, which protect against cancer and heart disease. As a prebiotic food, prunes also keep the digestive system healthy by increasing the colonization of friendly bacteria in the digestive system. They are a known laxative, too, thanks to the compound dihydroxyphenylisatin and their high fiber content. The fiber in prunes has other benefits—it has been shown to help protect against postmenopausal breast cancer, while the soluble form helps lower cholesterol. Prunes are a good source of iron, and also enable the iron we eat to become more easily absorbed.

- High antioxidant levels offer protection from the major diseases associated with aging.
- Prebiotic action keeps the digestive system healthy.
- Dihydroxyphenylisatin produces a laxative effect.
- Help iron absorption.

Practical tips:
Prunes can be softened or reconstituted by soaking in a little warm water or juice, or eaten as they are. Puree soft prunes in a blender and use in cake and dessert recipes to replace fat and/or sugar.

DID YOU KNOW?
California is one of the largest producers of prunes, and these producers are responsible for prunes being relabeled as dried plums—because of the constipation connection. It is thought that plums were first dried in the Mediterranean region several thousand years ago.

MAJOR NUTRIENTS PER 5 (1¾ oz.) PITTED PRUNES

Calories	120
Total fat	Trace
Protein	1 g
Carbohydrate	32 g
Fiber	3.5 g
Potassium	366 mg
Iron	0.5 mg
Beta-carotene	197 ug

Prune and walnut swirl cake

SERVES 12 (F) (M)

oil or melted butter, for greasing
20 pitted prunes
⅔ cup apple juice
1⅔ cups all-purpose white flour
2 teaspoons baking powder
1½ sticks unsalted butter, softened
¾ cup sugar
3 eggs, beaten
1 teaspoon vanilla extract
½ cup coarsely chopped walnuts

Method

1 Preheat the oven to 325°F. Grease and line a deep 7-inch square cake pan.

2 Place the prunes in a saucepan with the apple juice, bring to a boil, then reduce the heat and simmer for 8–10 minutes, until the liquid is absorbed. Put the prune mixture in a food processor or blender and process to a smooth, thick puree.

3 Sift the flour and baking powder into a large bowl and add the butter, sugar, eggs, and vanilla extract. Beat well until the batter is smooth. Reserve 2 tablespoons of the walnuts, then stir the remainder into the cake batter.

4 Spoon the batter into the prepared pan, then drop spoonfuls of the prune puree over the top of the batter. Swirl into the cake batter with a knife and smooth the surface level. Sprinkle the reserved walnuts over the top of the cake.

5 Bake in the preheated oven for 1–1 hour 10 minutes, or until risen, firm, and golden brown. Let cool in the pan for 10 minutes, then turn out and finish cooling on a wire rack. Cut the cake into squares to serve.

21 PEARS

Pears are one of the best fresh fruit sources of dietary fiber, and their low rating on the glycemic index makes them the perfect aid for weight control.

Pears contain one of the highest levels of dietary fiber of all fresh fruits. The insoluble fiber present in the flesh and skin helps keep the digestive system working efficiently and the bowels regular, while the soluble fiber helps to lower LDL blood cholesterol. The combination of fibers is one reason that pears are a good choice for women following lower-calorie diets or wanting to maintain a suitable weight. They are ideal for diabetics, for the same reason, and the fiber content appears to offer some protection against breast cancer, too. Pears also contain hydroxycinnamic acids, antioxidants that help boost the good bacteria in the digestive system and prevent digestive disorders, including irritable bowel syndrome (IBS). As a source of vitamin K, pears can help maintain strong bones and keep our arteries healthy as we age, and they are a good source of potassium, which controls fluid retention.

- Insoluble fiber content encourages healthy digestion and bowels.
- Contain hydroxycinnamic acids, useful for calming IBS.
- Low on the glycemic index, making them ideal for dieters.
- Dietary fiber may offer protection against breast cancer.

Practical tips:
Really ripe pears contain the most antioxidants. If possible, avoid peeling them because the antioxidants are mostly just under the skin, and the skin itself is an important source of fiber. Store away from strong smelling foods because they absorb odors easily.

DID YOU KNOW?
Pears are one of the few fruits to which hardly anyone seems to be allergic. As such, they are particularly useful for women whose fruit intake is restricted by allergy.

MAJOR NUTRIENTS PER AVERAGE-SIZE PEAR

Calories	60
Total fat	Trace
Protein	0.5 g
Carbohydrate	15 g
Fiber	3.3 g
Vitamin C	9 mg
Vitamin K	7 mg
Potassium	225 mg

Pear, walnut, and goat cheese salad

SERVES 4 ⓦ ⓑ ⓗ

4 pears, cored and cut into wedges
juice of ½ lemon
3 cups watercress or arugula
3 cups baby spinach
1 pound goat cheese with
   rind, sliced
½ cup walnut halves, toasted

Dressing
1½ tablespoons walnut oil
1½ tablespoons olive oil
½ teaspoon Dijon mustard
1 tablespoon white wine vinegar
½ teaspoon honey

Method

1 Preheat the broiler to high. To make the dressing, whisk together the walnut oil, olive oil, mustard, vinegar, and honey.

2 Heat a ridged grill pan until hot. Sprinkle the pear wedges with lemon juice, then cook them on the pan until they start to caramelize and have grill marks.

3 Divide the watercress and spinach leaves among four serving plates. Top with the pear wedges.

4 Cook the goat cheese under the preheated broiler until it starts to melt and turns golden.

5 Top each salad plate with goat cheese and sprinkle with toasted walnuts. Drizzle the dressing over the salad and serve immediately.

22 POMEGRANATE

Recent research has linked the regular consumption of pomegranate juice with a reduction in stress levels, a lower pulse rate, and improvement in mood and energy.

Other research has found that the fruit can reduce the symptoms of depression and increase libido. There is also anecdotal evidence to suggest that drinking pomegranate juice regularly may reduce the incidence and severity of hot flashes, the tendency to put on weight during menopause, and may also help to reduce high blood pressure. Both the juice and seeds contain some of the highest levels of antioxidants of any plant food, including the punicalagins—a type of tannin—anthocyanins and ellagic acid. These powerful compounds help limit the signs of aging, prevent cardiovascular disease, and reduce our risk of cancer and type 2 diabetes. Thanks to the estrogen-like compounds in the seeds, pomegranate also guards against the bone loss that accelerates during and after menopause.

- Regular consumption is linked with improvement in mood, libido, and energy levels.
- May reduce hot flashes and stress levels.
- May reduce abdominal fat and weight gain during menopause.
- High antioxidant levels fight disease and have antiaging properties.

Practical tips:
Halve the fruit and scoop out the seeds with a small spoon. The seeds can be sprinkled onto fruit salads or over savory salads, or onto yogurt or breakfast cereal.

DID YOU KNOW?

Pomegranate can interact with certain medications, such as some cholesterol-lowering drugs, and increase their effect. If you are taking medication, check with your doctor before enjoying pomegranate products.

MAJOR NUTRIENTS PER 1 CUP (3½ OZ.) EDIBLE POMEGRANATE

Calories	83
Total fat	1 g
Protein	1.7 g
Carbohydrate	18 g
Fiber	4 g
Potassium	236 mg
Vitamin C	10 mg
Folic acid	38 mcg

Pomegranate and passion fruit fizz

SERVES 1–2 (W) (F) (B) (H) (S)

1 pomegranate
½ small orange
4 passion fruit
½ cup sparkling mineral water

Method

1 Peel the rind from the pomegranate and peel the orange half, leaving on the white pith. Scoop the flesh from the passion fruit.
2 Put the pomegranate with the orange and pulp from 3 passion fruit in a fruit processor or blender and process until smooth.
3 Pour into glasses and stir in the remaining passion fruit pulp. Fill with the mineral water and serve.

23 RAISINS

These small, wrinkled fruits are the dried form of grapes. As concentrated sources of several nutrients, they are good to include in the diet around menopause.

Raisins are included in the top fifty foods known to supply the trace mineral boron in the diet. Boron is needed to convert estrogen—levels of which drop in females after menopause—to its most active form. This boosting of natural estrogen mimics the benefits of the contraceptive pill during menopause and may help to reduce symptoms, such as hot flashes, night sweats, and mood swings. Boron also encourages the absorption of vitamin D, which in turn lets the body utilize bone-forming calcium, thus helping to prevent osteoporosis. Raisins are a good source of the phenol catechin, known to help prevent colon cancer, and their high fiber content helps to lower blood cholesterol and prevent constipation. The high potassium content regulates blood pressure. Try raisins in place of candies, because they contain oleanolic acid, which provides protection against tooth decay and prevents the growth of harmful bacteria that can cause gum disease.

- Boron boosts estrogen levels and enables vitamin D to utilize calcium and strengthen bones.
- Rich in phenols, iron, and potassium.
- Oleanolic acid helps improve dental and gum health.

Practical tips:
Raisins are an ideal portable snack food. Choose organic raisins if possible—these have been dried without the help of sulfites, which can trigger an allergic reaction.

DID YOU KNOW?

In ancient Rome, raisins were used to garnish places of worship and were even used as prizes for winners in events, such as chariot racing.

MAJOR NUTRIENTS
PER 3 TBSP. (1 OZ.) RAISINS

Calories	75
Total fat	Trace
Protein	0.8 g
Carbohydrate	20 g
Fiber	1 g
Potassium	187 mg
Calcium	13 mg
Iron	0.5 mg
Fluoride	58 mcg

Raisin and cranberry granola

MAKES ABOUT 7 CUPS

(F) (S) (H) (M)

oil or melted butter, for greasing
2 tablespoons vegetable oil
½ cup maple syrup
3 tablespoons honey
3¼ cups rolled oats
¼ cup pumpkin seeds
¼ cup sunflower seeds
3 tablespoons sesame seeds
1 cup slivered almonds
½ cup dried flaked coconut
⅓ cup raisins
⅓ cup dried cranberries
fresh fruit and plain yogurt,
    to serve

Method

1   Preheat the oven to 300°F and grease 2 baking sheets.

2   Place the oil, maple syrup, and honey in a saucepan and heat gently until they all come together. Stir in the oats, seeds, and slivered almonds and mix together well.

3   Transfer the mixture to the prepared baking sheets and spread out evenly. Bake in the preheated oven for 15 minutes, then gently stir in the dried coconut, raisins, and dried cranberries. Bake for another 12–15 minutes.

4   Remove from the oven and pour onto a large baking sheet to cool. Store in an airtight jar or container.

5   Serve with fresh fruit and plain yogurt.

24 RASPBERRIES

Raspberries contain an antioxidant compound that helps minimize the signs of aging and the incidence of major diseases associated with midlife and older age.

Red raspberries rank highly on the ORAC scale. Their impressive antioxidant profile includes anthocyanins, the red/purple pigments that have been shown to help prevent heart disease and cancers and reduce the risk of varicose veins. Raspberries also contain high levels of ellagic acid, a compound that prevents damage to the cells of the body and can protect us against the signs of aging. Ellagic acid also helps reduce the incidence of breast cancer by minimizing the enzymes that let the cancer grow. Raspberries are high in vitamin C, too, which boosts the absorption of iron, also contained in the fruit, and co-enzyme Q-10, the "energy" enzyme, so they provide you with plenty of get-up-and-go. These delicious berries are high in fiber—both the soluble fiber pectin, which can lower blood cholesterol, and insoluble fiber, which helps keep the bowels regular.

- High antioxidant activity minimizes the signs of aging.
- Anthocyanins may help to prevent varicose veins.
- High in vitamin C and fiber, and a good source of iron.

Practical tips:
Raspberries are best eaten raw because cooking destroys some of their antioxidants. If you do cook them, poach them and serve them with their own juices. Raspberries freeze well and this retains their vitamin C.

DID YOU KNOW?

Although most raspberries we buy are red, they also come in white, pink, orange, and black varieties. The darker color berries contain the highest levels of antioxidants.

MAJOR NUTRIENTS PER ¾ CUP (3½ OZ.) RASPBERRIES

Calories	52
Total fat	0.6 g
Protein	1.2 g
Carbohydrate	12 g
Fiber	6.5 g
Vitamin C	26 mg
Vitamin B3	0.6 mg
Vitamin E	0.8 mg
Folic acid	21 mcg
Potassium	151 mg
Calcium	25 mg
Iron	0.7 mg
Zinc	0.4 mg

Grilled tropical fruit with raspberry sauce

SERVES 4 (W) (B) (H) (S)

2 mangoes, pitted, peeled,
  and cut into 4 cheeks
1 medium pineapple, peeled
  and cut into 8 wedges
2 tablespoons honey
mint sprigs, to garnish

Raspberry sauce

2½ cups raspberries
1 tablespoon confectioners' sugar
½ teaspoon lemon juice

Method

1 To make the raspberry sauce, place the raspberries, confectioners' sugar, and lemon juice in a food processor or blender and process until smooth. Push through a strainer, then check for sweetness. Depending on the ripeness of the raspberries, you may want to add more sugar or lemon juice.

2 Place the prepared fruit in a bowl and pour the honey over them. Let marinate for 20 minutes, turning occasionally.

3 Heat a ridged grill pan until hot and cook the fruit for 10–12 minutes, turning occasionally, until it starts to caramelize. Pour over any excess honey while the fruit is cooking.

4 Divide the grilled fruit among four serving plates. Serve immediately with the raspberry sauce on the side and mint sprigs sprinkled over.

25

STRAWBERRIES

Thanks to the high level of vitamin C they contain, strawberries can give a powerful boost to your immune system during this more vulnerable time.

Strawberries are extremely rich in the antioxidant vitamin C— an average portion contains a whole day's recommended daily amount for an adult. Vitamin C boosts the immune system, prevents heart disease, and enhances mood and memory. It also improves skin and gum condition and helps the body to absorb energy-boosting iron, utilize the energy-giving co-enzyme Q-10, and burn calories. Strawberries also contain other antioxidant compounds in good amounts, including anthocyanins and ellagic acid (found in the highest amounts in the red outer layer), which help protect against cancer. Several recent studies have found that eating strawberries regularly decreases the risk of type 2 diabetes, possibly because of the presence of a particular family of plant compounds called ellagitannins. In addition to all this, they contain dietary fiber to help lower blood cholesterol, folic acid for a healthy heart, and potassium to minimize fluid retention.

- Vitamin C content promotes good skin, memory, and energy.
- Ellagic acid and anthocyanins protect against cancer.
- Ellagitannins may help to decrease the risk of type 2 diabetes.
- Contain fiber, which helps lower LDL blood cholesterol.

Practical tips:

Choose bright red and glossy strawberries for maximum nutrient content. Remove the leaf just before using; only slice if necessary, at the last minute, because cutting destroys their vitamin C.

DID YOU KNOW?

In folk medicine across the world, strawberries have been recommended as a cure for everything from alcohol poisoning to headaches and halitosis.

MAJOR NUTRIENTS PER ⅔ CUP (3½ OZ.) STRAWBERRIES

Calories	32
Total fat	0.3 g
Protein	0.7 g
Carbohydrate	7.7 g
Fiber	2 g
Vitamin C	59 mg
Potassium	153 mg
Folic acid	24 mcg
Lutein/Zeaxanthin	26 mcg

Mini strawberry cheesecakes

MAKES 6   (B) (M)

6 tablespoons unsalted butter
¾ cup rolled oats
¼ cup chopped hazelnuts
1 cup ricotta cheese
¼ cup demerara sugar or other
    raw sugar
finely grated rind of 1 lemon,
    and juice of ½ lemon
1 egg, plus 1 egg yolk
⅔ cup cottage cheese
1 kiwi
3 large strawberries

Method

1 Line 6 cups of a muffin pan with baking cups.

2 Melt the butter in a small saucepan over low heat, then let cool. Put the oats in a food processor or blender and blend briefly to break them up, then transfer to a bowl, add the nuts and melted butter, and mix well. Divide the batter among the baking cups and press down well. Chill for 30 minutes.

3 Preheat the oven to 300°F. Beat the ricotta cheese with the sugar, lemon rind, and lemon juice in a bowl. Add the egg, egg yolk, and cottage cheese and mix well. Spoon into the baking cups and bake in the preheated oven for 30 minutes. Turn off the oven, but let the cheesecakes rest in the oven until completely cold.

4 Peel the kiwi and slice into circles. Halve the strawberries. Remove the baking cups, top each cheesecake with the fruit, and serve.

26 ORANGES

Oranges are one of the best sources of vitamin C and plant compounds to supercharge your immune system and challenge many of the signs of aging.

Vitamin C not only helps to protect our bodies from the cell damage that causes aging and disease, but can also improve mood, memory, and skin, helps keep gums healthy, and improves calcium and iron absorption. Oranges are also a good source of pectin, a soluble fiber known to help control blood cholesterol levels. Meanwhile, our intake of calcium, vital for bone maintenance, gets a helping hand from the folic acid and potassium they contain. Oranges also contain rutin, a flavonoid that can help slow down or prevent the growth of tumors, nobiletin, an anti-inflammatory compound, and naringenin, a flavonoid that may help lower cholesterol. All these plant compounds help vitamin C to work more effectively. Red-pigmented "blood" oranges contain particularly good levels of antioxidants in the form of anthocyanin pigments, which are linked to cancer prevention.

- Good source of vitamin C, which protects against the cell damage that can cause aging and disease.
- Contain a range of flavonoids that help lower cholesterol.

Practical tips:
Keep oranges in a refrigerator where they will not be exposed to heat or light and so retain their vitamin C content. Eat some of the white pith and peel, as well as the flesh, because these contain high levels of fiber and the plant chemicals (if eating the peel, wash well or buy organic fruit).

DID YOU KNOW?
One extensive four-year study found that eating an orange a day may reduce your risk of death in midlife by as much as twenty percent.

MAJOR NUTRIENTS PER AVERAGE-SIZE ORANGE

Calories	65
Total fat	Trace
Protein	1g
Carbohydrate	16 g
Fiber	3.4 g
Vitamin C	64 mg
Potassium	238 mg
Calcium	61 mg

Red bell pepper and orange soup

SERVES 4 (W) (B) (H) (S)

5 blood oranges
3 tablespoons olive oil
12 red bell peppers (about
    3¼ pounds), seeded and sliced
1½ tablespoons orange flower
    water
salt and pepper
extra virgin olive oil, for drizzling
    (optional)

Method

1 Finely grate the rind of one of the oranges and shred the rind of
another with a citrus zester. Set aside. Squeeze the juice from
all the oranges.

2 Heat the oil in a saucepan over medium heat. Add the bell peppers
and cook, stirring occasionally, for 10 minutes. Stir in the grated
orange rind and cook for an additional few minutes. Reduce the
heat, cover, and simmer gently, stirring occasionally, for 20 minutes.

3 Remove the pan from the heat, let cool slightly, then transfer the bell
pepper mixture to a food processor or blender and process to a
smooth puree. Add the orange juice and orange flower water and
process again until thoroughly combined.

4 Transfer the soup to a bowl, season with salt and pepper, and let
cool completely, then cover with plastic wrap and chill in the
refrigerator for 3 hours. Stir well before serving, then sprinkle with
shredded orange rind and drizzle olive oil over the soup, if using.

Vegetables

While vegetables are a vital part of our diets throughout our lives, they are even more valuable during and after menopause. A range of vegetables—root, bulb, leaf, stem, or pod—in different colors provides not only exciting plant chemicals that can minimize negative symptoms but also a huge variety of nutrients.

(W) Ideal for weight control

(F) High in fiber

(B) Protects and strengthens bones

(H) Heart health

(M) Mood booster

(S) Improves skin condition

27

BEET

Rich in plant compounds that safeguard our health, and high in several important vitamins and minerals, beet makes a tasty and nutritious addition to the diet.

Beets contain plant compounds called betalains that are strongly antioxidant and help to keep the heart, arteries, and tissue healthy and free from cancers. Betalains are also anti-inflammatory, so they can help prevent diseases, such as arthritis, and they are detoxifying, which makes beets a good choice in a midlife detox or dieting program. Beets are rich in the carotenes lutein and zeaxanthin, which boost eye health and help ward off age-related eye problems, such as macular degeneration. They are also rich in folic acid, the B vitamin that can help reduce levels of the dangerous amino acid homocysteine in the blood. In addition, beets are high in potassium, which acts as a natural diuretic; are a good source of soluble and insoluble fibers, which are vital for digestive health; contain magnesium to support the bones and heart; and have iron for energy and brain function.

- Unique betalain content offers a range of health benefits during menopause.
- A detoxifying and diuretic root that is ideal for dieters.
- Contains lutein and zeaxanthin for eyesight protection.
- Rich in folic acid, so able to reduce harmful homocysteine levels.

DID YOU KNOW?

The dark-green purple-tinged leaves of the root are an edible vegetable, too, and can be sliced and steamed. Like the root, they are rich in vitamins, minerals, and carotenes.

MAJOR NUTRIENTS PER ¾ CUP (3½ OZ.) WHOLE BEETS

Calories	36
Protein	1.7 g
Total fat	Trace
Carbohydrate	7.6 g
Fiber	1.9 g
Vitamin C	5 mg
Folic acid	150 mcg
Potassium	380 mg
Calcium	20 mg
Iron	1.0 mg
Magnesium	23 mg

Practical tips:
Boil or steam beets whole—leave the skin on to prevent loss of the valuable red juices and peel afterward. Raw beet can be grated in place of carrot in a slaw salad.

Beet hummus

SERVES 4–6 (**W**) (**F**) (**H**)

1 (15-ounce) can chickpeas,
    drained and rinsed
1 garlic clove, coarsely chopped
2 cooked beets
1½ tablespoons tahini
juice of ½ lemon
3 tablespoons olive oil
salt and pepper
vegetable sticks and cherry
    tomatoes, to serve

Method

1 Place the chickpeas, garlic, and beets in a food processor or blender and process until broken into crumbs.
2 Add the tahini and lemon juice and process again, pouring in the olive oil until the hummus is the consistency you like. Season with salt and pepper.
3 Serve the hummus with vegetable sticks and cherry tomatoes.

ASPARAGUS

Asparagus spears contain an impressive range of nutrients and chemicals that can help alleviate menopausal symptoms from hot flashes to low moods.

Asparagus is one of the few good vegetable sources of vitamin E, which helps reduce the severity of hot flashes, and is also a source of calcium, magnesium, and vitamin K, which keep our bones healthy. As well as a good range of all the B vitamins, which work to lift our mood and combat depression, asparagus contains several anti-inflammatory nutrients, which if consumed regularly, reduce the risk of heart disease, rheumatoid arthritis, and some cancers. The high fiber content of asparagus makes it a useful food for dieters and to help manage type 2 diabetes. It is a valuable source of vitamin C and iron, too, which improve concentration, mood, and our energy levels. Asparagus is rich in inulin and a type of soluble fiber called oligosaccharide, both of which act as prebiotics in the digestive tract, stimulating the growth of "friendly" bacteria that keep the digestive system healthy.

- Antioxidants provide general disease prevention.
- Contains a range of vitamins, including vitamin E, which helps calm hot flashes.
- Calcium, magnesium, and vitamin K for healthy bones.
- Ideal low-calorie food that will prevent weight gain.

Practical tips:
For taste, texture, and nutrient content, eat as soon as possible after picking. Cook spears of the same size, stem ends down, in a small saucepan in a little water. Young asparagus tips can be eaten raw.

DID YOU KNOW?

Wild asparagus has long been used in India and much of Asia for its medicinal properties. Even in cultivated form, it has been around for over 2,000 years.

MAJOR NUTRIENTS PER 5 LARGE (3½ oz.) ASPARAGUS SPEARS

Calories	20
Protein	2.2 g
Total fat	Trace
Carbohydrate	3.9 g
Fiber	2.1 g
Vitamin C	5.6 g
Vitamin E	1.1 g
Folic acid	52 mcg
Vitamin K	41.6 mcg
Potassium	202 mg
Calcium	24 mg
Magnesium	14 mg
Iron	2 mg

Asparagus with poached eggs and Parmesan

SERVES 4 　Ⓦ Ⓕ Ⓑ Ⓗ Ⓜ

20 asparagus spears (about
　12 ounces), trimmed
4 extra-large eggs
1 cup Parmesan cheese shavings
pepper

Method

1　Bring two saucepans of water to a boil. Add the asparagus to one saucepan, return to a simmer, and cook for 5 minutes, or until just tender.

2　Meanwhile, reduce the heat of the second saucepan to a simmer and carefully crack in the eggs, one at a time. Poach for 3 minutes, or until the whites are just set but the yolks are still soft. Remove with a slotted spoon.

3　Drain the asparagus and divide among four serving plates. Top each plate of asparagus with an egg and top with the Parmesan cheese. Season with pepper and serve immediately.

BOK CHOY

Bok choy, or Chinese cabbage, belongs to the same family as broccoli and kale, and is almost as rich in nutrients for bone maintenance and disease protection.

Bok choy is high in glucosinolates and other plant compounds that break down in the body into indoles, which help to slow down the growth of cancers and protect the cells from damage against free radicals. It is one of the richest vegetable sources of calcium, the mineral vital for the maintenance and repair of bones during and after menopause. It also contains a good amount of vitamin K and magnesium, both of which work with calcium to increase bone density. Bok choy is especially high in vitamin C, and you can get your whole day's recommended intake in one medium-to-large portion. Vitamin C gives a boost to the collagen underlying our skin, keeping it firm, and improves our mood. Bok choy is also low in calories, yet a good source of fiber and potassium, making it a sensible choice for people who want to lose weight and/or who have problems with fluid retention.

- Rich in cancer-preventing plant compounds, including indoles.
- High in calcium and also a good source of vitamin K and magnesium, which strengthens bones.
- Contains vitamin C for boosting collagen.
- Good choice for dieters.

Practical tips:
Bok choy is delicious sliced and used in a stir-fry, or steamed with broiled meats. Store it in a plastic food bag in the refrigerator. Don't wash the leaves before storage or they will turn mushy.

DID YOU KNOW?
The glucosinolate compounds in bok choy have anticancer effects when consumed in small amounts but are toxic to humans in large doses. The thyroid gland may swell if your intake regularly exceeds 2¼ pounds a day.

MAJOR NUTRIENTS PER 7 LEAVES (3½ oz.) BOK CHOY

Calories	13
Protein	1.5 g
Total fat	0.2 g
Carbohydrate	2 g
Fiber	1 g
Vitamin C	45 mg
Folic acid	66 mcg
Vitamin K	45 mcg
Beta-carotene	2,681 mcg
Potassium	252 mg
Calcium	105 mg
Iron	0.8 mg
Magnesium	19 mg

Tofu and bok choy stir-fry

SERVES 4   (W)(F)(B)(H)(M)

2 tablespoons sunflower or olive oil

2 cups drained and cubed firm tofu

3 cups coarsely chopped bok choy

1 garlic clove, chopped

2 tablespoons sweet chili sauce

2 tablespoons light soy sauce

Method

1 Heat 1 tablespoon of oil in a wok, add the tofu in batches, and stir-fry for 2–3 minutes, until golden. Remove and set aside.

2 Add the bok choy to the wok and stir-fry for a few seconds, until tender and wilted. Remove from the wok and set aside.

3 Add the remaining oil to the wok, then add the garlic and stir-fry for 30 seconds. Stir in the chili sauce and soy sauce and bring to a boil.

4 Return the tofu and bok choy to the wok and toss gently until coated in the sauce. Serve immediately.

30

CELERY

Celery stalks can help you maintain a reasonable body weight throughout life because they have a low calorie content and take a long time to digest.

The high fiber and water content in celery stalks keeps the stomach feeling full for a long time. Celery is also a good source of potassium, a mineral that helps to prevent fluid retention and stomach bloating. It also contains some calcium, which is vital for healthy bones and for maintaining healthy blood pressure levels. Recent research has found that celery also contains luteolin, a compound that can help prevent memory loss as we get older. The antioxidant compounds it provides us with, called coumarins, help prevent free radicals from damaging the body cells. This action reduces the likelihood of cancers developing in the body. Celery also contains the compounds polyacetylenes and phthalides, which may protect us from inflammatory conditions, such as arthritis, and high blood pressure.

- Low calories and high fiber content helps regulate body weight.
- Can help minimize fluid retention.
- Offers protection from memory loss and inflammatory diseases, such as arthritis.

Practical tips:
Raw celery stalks take longer to digest than when eaten cooked. Celery is ideal for adding volume without many calories to casseroles. Leaves can be added to salads or used as a garnish.

DID YOU KNOW?

To prevent celery stalks from wilting and losing their crisp texture, keep them together on the "head" until use. If you do have to keep single stalks, put them in a plastic bag in the crisper compartment of the refrigerator.

MAJOR NUTRIENTS PER 2½ MEDIUM (3½ oz.) CELERY STALKS

Calories	14
Protein	0.7 g
Total fat	Trace
Carbohydrate	3 g
Fiber	1.6 g
Vitamin C	3 mg
Folic acid	36 mcg
Vitamin K	35 mcg
Potassium	260 mg
Calcium	40 mg
Magnesium	11 mg

Gazpacho with celery salsa

SERVES 2 (**W**) (**H**) (**S**)

2 thick slices day-old fresh white
*   bread, crusts removed*
½ cup water, for soaking
4 tomatoes, seeded and skinned
1 small cucumber, peeled, seeded,
*   and chopped*
1 red bell pepper, seeded and
*   chopped*
1 large red chile, seeded and
*   finely chopped*
1 large garlic clove
3 tablespoons olive oil
juice of 1 lemon
pepper

Celery salsa

1 celery stalk, sliced
1 small avocado, skinned,
*   pitted, and diced*
6 large basil leaves

Method

1 Soak one of the slices of bread in the water for 5 minutes.
2 Put the bread, tomatoes and any juices, cucumber, red bell pepper, three-quarters of the chile, the garlic, 1 tablespoon of the oil, and the lemon juice (reserving 1 teaspoon) in a food processor or blender and process until combined but still a little chunky. Season with pepper, then chill for 2–3 hours.
3 Just before serving, make the celery salsa. Put the celery, avocado, reserved lemon juice, basil, and remaining chile in a bowl and stir until combined.
4 Cut the second slice of bread into cubes. Heat the remaining olive oil in a skillet and sauté the bread for about 5 minutes, or until golden and crisp.
5 Ladle the soup into serving bowls and top with a large spoonful of the salsa and the croutons.

31

BRUSSELS SPROUTS

Sprouts provide menopausal women with a range of health-giving nutrients. They offer high protection levels against cancers due to their sulfur content.

Brussels sprouts are members of the brassica family and one of our most potent weapons against illness during midlife and old age. Studies show that women who eat a lot of sprouts have a much lower risk of several types of cancer, including breast cancer. The anticancer effect is due to bioflavonoids, carotenes, and indoles, which have an anti-estrogenic action. Sprouts also contain a high level of vitamin C—150 percent of your recommended daily intake in just one portion. Vitamin C is a strong antioxidant, and keeps the heart and arteries healthy as well as gives a boost to the collagen under our skin. It also helps the mineral iron—present in high quantities in brussels sprouts—to be absorbed in the body, giving you maximum energy and brain capability. Sprouts also contain selenium, which is known to help fight cancer and depression and may even improve libido.

- Indoles help protect against breast cancer, while other compounds protect against different cancers.
- High in vitamin C for heart protection and younger-looking skin.
- Rich in iron to give you increased energy and brain power.

Practical tips:
Fresh brussels sprouts contain the highest nutrient levels. Choose bright green, almost glossy sprouts with no sign of yellowing on the outer leaves. To retain nutrients, cook them by lightly steaming until still a little firm, refresh in cold water, and serve immediately.

DID YOU KNOW?

Brussels sprouts—so named because they were first used as a kitchen vegetable in Belgium—are one of our newest cooking vegetables, because they have only been used widely for about a hundred years.

MAJOR NUTRIENTS PER 5 (3½ oz.) BRUSSELS SPROUTS

Calories	43
Protein	3.5 g
Total fat	0.3 g
Carbohydrate	9 g
Fiber	3.8 g
Vitamin C	85 mg
Folic acid	61 mcg
Potassium	389 mg
Magnesium	23 mg
Calcium	42 mg
Iron	1.4 mg
Selenium	1.6 mcg
Zinc	0.4 mg

Sautéed brussels sprouts

SERVES 4   (**W**)(**F**)(**H**)(**S**)

2½ tablespoons olive oil

2 strips unsmoked bacon, diced

1 pound brussels sprouts, cut in
    half lengthwise

4 shallots, diced

½ cup vegetable stock

juice of ½ lemon

pepper

¼ cup Parmesan cheese shavings,
    to serve

Method

1 Heat the olive oil in a large skillet over medium heat and sauté the
   bacon for 2–3 minutes.

2 Add the sprouts, cut-side down, and sprinkle the shallots over
   them. Cook the sprouts for about 5 minutes, then turn them over
   and cook for another 5 minutes on the other side.

3 Pour the vegetable stock over the sprouts and steam-fry until the
   liquid has been absorbed and the sprouts are tender.

4 Transfer to a serving dish and sprinkle with lemon juice and pepper.
   Serve immediately with Parmesan cheese shavings.

32

CABBAGE

On a cost-per-serving basis, cabbage is one of our most economical sources of beneficial plant chemicals, antioxidants, vitamins, and minerals.

All cabbages are a good source of vitamin C. They are rich in vitamin K and are a reasonable source of calcium, both of which offer bone protection. They also contain a type of fiber that binds with fat in the digestive system to help lower blood cholesterol, and lignans to help reduce the symptoms of hot flashes. Cabbage is low on the glycemic index and low in calories, so it is an ideal food for dieters. Dark green varieties, such as savoy and collard greens, have the most valuable plant compounds. All dark-leaved cabbages are rich in indoles, which protect the body from breast cancer, and monoterpenes, which protect aging cells from free radical damage. Red cabbage contains even higher levels of the anti-inflammatory pigments anthocyanin and lycopene to fight against memory loss and Alzheimer's disease.

- Lignan content can help reduce the severity of hot flashes.
- Contains compounds to help fight aging, cancer, and memory loss.
- Low in calories and low on the glycemic index.
- Vitamin K and calcium to promote bone health.

Practical tips:
Use thinly sliced raw red cabbage in coleslaw instead of green cabbage. Sprinkle with lemon juice to prevent the cabbage from turning gray. Cut the cabbage just before use; once cut, the leaves begin to lose vitamin C. Cook by steaming to preserve nutrients.

DID YOU KNOW?
Cabbage is a source of the important omega-3 fat alpha linolenic acid, which the body can convert into the omega-3 fats EPA and DHA, found in oily fish. This makes it a useful food for vegetarians.

MAJOR NUTRIENTS PER 1⅓ CUPS CHOPPED (3½ OZ.) CABBAGE

Calories	31
Protein	1.2 g
Total fat	Trace
Carbohydrate	5.3 g
Fiber	2.3 g
Vitamin C	57 mg
Folic acid	18 mcg
Niacin	0.4 mg
Vitamin K	76 mcg
Potassium	243 mg
Calcium	45 mg
Iron	0.8 mg
Selenium	0.6 mcg
Beta-carotene	670 mcg

Mixed cabbage coleslaw

SERVES 4 (**W**) (**B**) (**H**)

1 cup finely shredded red cabbage

1 cup finely shredded white
    cabbage (or green cabbage if
    white cabbage is not available)

½ cup finely shredded green
    cabbage

2 carrots, shredded

1 white onion, finely sliced

2 red apples, chopped

¼ cup orange juice

2 celery stalks, finely sliced

⅓ cup drained, canned
    corn kernels

2 tablespoons raisins

Dressing

¼ cup low-fat plain yogurt

1 tablespoon chopped
    fresh parsley

pepper

Method

1 Place the cabbages in a bowl and stir in the carrots and onion.
Toss the apples in the orange juice and add to the cabbages
together with any remaining orange juice, the celery, corn, and
raisins. Mix well.

2 To make the dressing, put the yogurt and parsley in a bowl, season
with pepper, mix together, then pour it over the cabbage mixture.
Stir and serve.

33 CARROTS

Carrots are rich in carotenes—antioxidants that help protect us from breast cancer, cardiovascular disease, and eye problems, and keep skin young and lungs healthy.

Carrots are one of the lowest in calories of the root vegetables and yet the most nutrient-rich. Inexpensive and widely available all year round, they are an excellent source of antioxidant compounds, particularly alpha- and beta-carotene, which gives them their orange color. It is the antioxidants in carrots that help protect us against heart disease and strokes, breast and other cancers, and lung disease. Two in particular, lutein and zeaxanthin, protect eyesight. Carotenes are thought to reduce heart disease in humans by around 45 percent and stroke by up to 70 percent. They are highly beneficial for older skin, too, because they protect against sun damage, and help prevent the oxidation that is a major cause of skin aging. Carotenes are also believed to improve concentration and memory.

- High carotene content protects against heart disease, stroke, and breast cancer.
- Provide protection against skin aging and sun damage, and also for our eyesight.
- An aid to memory and concentration.

Practical tips:
The carotenes in carrots are more easily absorbed if the carrots are cooked and eaten with a little fat, such as olive oil. The darker orange the carrot, the more carotenes it will contain. The green part of the root near the stem is mildly toxic, so do not eat.

DID YOU KNOW?

Eating large portions of carrots regularly can give the skin a light tan appearance. This effect is called carotenemia and is harmless. Eating carrots also helps the skin to tan safely in the sun.

MAJOR NUTRIENTS PER 2 SMALL (3½ oz.) CARROTS

Calories	41
Protein	0.9 g
Total fat	Trace
Carbohydrate	9.6 g
Fiber	2.8 g
Vitamin C	6 mg
Vitamin E	0.7 mg
Beta-carotene	8,285 mcg
Calcium	33 mg
Potassium	320 mg
Lutein/Zeaxanthin	256 mcg

Zucchini, carrot, and tomato frittata

SERVES 4 (**W**) (**H**) (**S**)

1 tablespoon olive oil

1 onion, cut into small wedges

1–2 garlic cloves, crushed

2 eggs

2 egg whites

1 zucchini, shredded

2 carrots, shredded

2 tomatoes, chopped

pepper

1 tablespoon shredded fresh basil, for sprinkling

Method

1 Heat the olive oil in a large nonstick skillet over medium heat, add the onion and garlic, and sauté for 5 minutes, stirring frequently. Beat together the eggs and egg whites in a bowl, then pour into the skillet. Using a spatula or fork, pull the egg mixture from the sides of the skillet into the center, letting the uncooked egg take its place.

2 Once the bottom has set lightly, add the zucchini and carrots with the tomatoes. Season with pepper and continue to cook over low heat until the eggs are set to personal preference.

3 Transfer to serving plates. Sprinkle with the shredded basil, cut the frittata into quarters, and serve hot or cold.

SWEET POTATO

Sweet potato is a much more nutritious choice of starchy carbohydrate than the standard potato. It is high in carotenes and cholesterol-lowering compounds.

MAJOR NUTRIENTS PER 1 (5½ oz.) SWEET POTATO

Calories	129
Protein	2.4 g
Total fat	Trace
Carbohydrate	30.2 g
Fiber	4.5 g
Vitamin C	3.6 mg
Vitamin E	0.4 mg
Potassium	506 mg
Calcium	45 mg
Iron	0.9 mg
Magnesium	38 mg
Zinc	0.5 mg
Selenium	0.9 mcg
Beta-carotene	12,760 mcg

Sweet potatoes are lower on the glycemic index than standard potatoes and so are of benefit for diabetics and dieters. They are rich in anthocyanins, the heart-friendly antioxidant pigments. Sweet potatoes also contain plant sterols and the soluble fiber pectin, which can help lower LDL blood cholesterol. They are extremely high in beta-carotene, too. This antioxidant may help to prevent breast and other cancers and boost the immune system. Sweet potatoes are also a source of vitamin E, which can improve skin condition as well as reduce the duration or frequency of hot flashes. Eating sweet potato will also provide you with several minerals, including magnesium, which works with calcium to keep your bones healthy, and selenium, which can help improve your skin and mood. A useful amount of calcium is provided as well, to help prevent osteoporosis and bone loss.

- Low on the glycemic index, so ideal for dieters and diabetics.
- Vitamin E helps improve dry skin and other skin conditions and may reduce the incidence and severity of hot flashes.
- Carotenes may help prevent cancers and also heart disease.
- Sterols and pectin content help reduce LDL cholesterol.

Practical tips:
Use as you would ordinary potatoes: peeled and cut into chunks and then steamed or boiled; baked whole; peeled and roasted; or as fries. Serve with a little olive oil to help carotene absorption.

Baked sweet potatoes with red pepper hummus

SERVES 6　(**W**)(**H**)(**M**)(**S**)

6 orange-fleshed sweet potatoes,
　unpeeled
olive oil
sea salt
chopped fresh flat-leaf parsley,
　to garnish
salad greens, to serve

Red pepper hummus

1 (15-ounce) can chickpeas,
　drained and rinsed
juice of 2 lemons
⅓ cup tahini
2 tablespoons olive oil
1 garlic clove, crushed
½ cup drained and sliced roasted
　red peppers in olive oil
salt and pepper

Method

1 Preheat the oven to 425°F. Use a fork to pierce the sweet
potatoes all over, then rub with the olive oil and sprinkle with salt.
Place the sweet potatoes directly on an oven rack and roast for
35–45 minutes, until they are tender when pierced with a knife.

2 Meanwhile, make the red pepper hummus. Put the chickpeas and
2 tablespoons of the lemon juice in a food processor or blender
and process until a thick paste forms. Add the tahini, olive oil, and
garlic and process again. Add the roasted red peppers, season with
salt and pepper, and process again. Taste and add extra lemon
juice, if desired. Scrape into a bowl, cover with plastic wrap, and
chill until required.

3 When the potatoes are tender, slit each one lengthwise and
squeeze open. Top each potato with a good spoonful of red
pepper hummus, garnish with the parsley, and serve with some
salad greens.

35 BEAN SPROUTS

The health benefits of beans are at their highest in sprout form, and, therefore, bean sprouts are a valuable addition to the diet during menopause.

Bean sprouts have been a traditional Asian remedy for menopausal symptoms for many years. Alfalfa, soy, and mung bean sprouts, in particular, are thought to relieve symptoms, such as hot flashes, night sweats, and mood swings, because they are rich in coumestrol, a plant compound that has estrogen-like effects, and in the isoflavones genistein and daidzein, which are also estrogenic. Bean sprouts are ideal to help weight control because they are low in calories and high in fiber. They are a good source of pantothenic acid, a type of B vitamin that can help prevent fatigue, and other B vitamins, which may control depression.

- Estrogenic compounds can help minimize hot flashes, night sweats, and mood swings.
- An ideal food for weight control, being low calorie and high fiber.
- B vitamins may help beat fatigue and depression.
- Rich in antioxidant minerals that provide a range of benefits.

Practical tips:
Raw bean sprouts contain the maximum amounts of the B vitamins and vitamin C. Lightly stir-fry in peanut oil or olive oil, or steam for a minute and serve instead of potatoes or pasta. Bean sprouts are best kept in the refrigerator and eaten on the day of purchase. Be aware that the process of germinating seeds for sprouts is conducive to bacterial growth and has resulted in outbreaks of food-borne illness.

DID YOU KNOW?

Bean sprouts are easy to digest, even raw, because the enzymes they contain help to break down the proteins and fats contained in the sprouts.

MAJOR NUTRIENTS PER 3 CUPS (5 OZ.) ALFALFA SPROUTS

Calories	23
Protein	4 g
Total fat	0.7 g
Carbohydrate	2 g
Fiber	2 g
Vitamin C	8 mg
Niacin	0.5 mg
Pantothenic acid	0.6 mg
Vitamin K	30.5 mcg
Choline	14.5 mg
Calcium	32 mg
Magnesium	27 mg
Iron	1 mg
Zinc	0.9 mg

Stir-fried bean sprouts

SERVES 4   (W) (F) (M)

1 tablespoon peanut oil or olive oil

2½ cups bean sprouts

2 tablespoons finely chopped
    scallion

½ teaspoon salt

pinch of sugar

Method

1 In a preheated wok or deep saucepan, heat the oil and stir-fry the
   bean sprouts with the scallion for about 1 minute. Add the salt and
   sugar and stir.

2 Remove from the heat and serve immediately.

36 CAULIFLOWER

This member of the brassica family contains several powerful antioxidants and plant compounds that offer protection against menopausal symptoms.

Studies show that the indole compounds in cauliflower can protect women from breast and ovarian cancer. These same compounds appear to help protect women from the unwanted symptoms of menopause, such as hot flashes and night sweats, by helping to regulate hormones. One molecule in cauliflower, indole-3-carbinol, is a powerful anti-inflammatory, which may help to prevent arthritis, heart disease, and cancers. Another glucosinolate, glucoraphanin, can be converted into sulforaphane, which not only helps prevent, but may even reverse, the signs of arterial disease. Glucosinolates, in general, are being investigated for their ability to help prevent or control irritable bowel syndrome (IBS), obesity, and type 2 diabetes. Cauliflower is also high in potassium, which is a diuretic, vitamin C, and fiber, as well as choline, which prevents the buildup of harmful homocysteine in the blood.

- Indoles protect against breast and ovarian cancers.
- Regulates hormones and helps minimize menopausal symptoms.
- Compounds that protect against heart and arterial disease.
- May help combat diabetes.

Practical tips:
Serve small, tender florets raw for dipping in condiments. To cook, divide into florets and steam for only a few minutes to retain the vitamins. Use cauliflower within two days of purchase. If there is brown spotting on the flowerhead, it is past its best.

DID YOU KNOW?
Although the "curd," or head—which is actually the undeveloped flowers of the plant—is the part most often eaten, the stalks and the leaves of cauliflower are also edible and contain similar nutrients.

MAJOR NUTRIENTS PER ¾ CUP (3½ OZ.) FLORETS

Calories	25
Protein	1.9 g
Total fat	0.3 g
Carbohydrate	5 g
Fiber	2 g
Vitamin C	48 mg
Folic acid	57 mcg
Vitamin B6	0.2 mg
Vitamin K	15.5 mcg
Potassium	299 mg
Calcium	22 mg
Iron	0.4 mg
Choline	44 mg

Cauliflower and beans with cashew nuts

SERVES 4 Ⓦ Ⓗ Ⓜ

1 tablespoon vegetable oil or
    peanut oil
1 tablespoon chili oil
1 onion, chopped
2 garlic cloves, chopped
2 tablespoons Thai red curry paste
1 small head of cauliflower,
    cut into florets
1½ cups 3-inch-long green bean
    pieces
⅔ cup vegetable stock
2 tablespoons Thai soy sauce
⅓ cup cashew nuts, toasted,
    to garnish

Method

1 Heat both the oils in a wok and stir-fry the onion and garlic until softened. Add the curry paste and stir-fry for 1–2 minutes.

2 Add the cauliflower and beans and stir-fry for 3–4 minutes, until softened. Pour in the stock and soy sauce and simmer for 1–2 minutes. Serve immediately, garnished with the cashew nuts.

37 FENNEL

The fennel bulb is rich in a wide range of health-giving vitamins, minerals, and plant nutrients, making it great news for menopausal health.

Fennel is ideal for women who are watching their weight because it is low in calories but, because of its crunchy texture, it also takes a long time to eat, helping us to feel full. Its high fiber content contributes to satiety, while its high potassium content helps eliminate fluid, which keeps us feeling slim and controls high blood pressure. The juice of fennel is said to eliminate toxins from the body and has traditionally been used to relieve bloating and gas. The bulb is high in calcium for bone health. Fennel is a good source of beta-carotene, too, which protects the skin from sunburn and aging. Its main plant compound is anethole, which can reduce inflammation and may, therefore, help to minimize the symptoms of arthritis and to prevent heart disease and cancers.

- Good choice of low-calorie, high-fiber food for weight watchers.
- Can relieve bloating, indigestion, and gas.
- Calcium can help improve and protect bone health.
- Helps protect skin from sunburn and reduce symptoms of arthritis.

Practical tips:

Fennel bulb is probably best eaten raw, sliced with a little olive oil poured over it—the oil helps the plant chemicals to be absorbed. Fennel can also be braised in stock or cut into thick slices and roasted in oil. Fennel goes well with fish and chicken. All parts of the plant are edible, and the leaves make a tasty garnish.

DID YOU KNOW?

Fennel has been used by both the Greeks and Romans for thousands of years as a herbal medicine to cure coughs and poor digestion, and as a diuretic and detoxifier.

MAJOR NUTRIENTS PER 1 CUP SLICED (3½ OZ.) FENNEL

Calories	31
Protein	1.3 g
Total fat	0.2 g
Carbohydrate	7.3 g
Fiber	3 g
Vitamin C	12 mg
Folic acid	42 mcg
Magnesium	17 mg
Potassium	414 mg
Calcium	49 mg
Iron	0.7 mg

Fennel and tomato soup with shrimp

SERVES 4   (**W**) (**B**) (**H**) (**S**)

2 teaspoons olive oil
1 large onion, halved and sliced
2 large fennel bulbs, halved
    and sliced
1 small potato, peeled and diced
3½ cups water
1¾ cups tomato juice,
    plus extra if needed
1 bay leaf
4 ounces cooked, peeled
    small shrimp
2 tomatoes, skinned,
    seeded, and chopped
½ teaspoon snipped fresh dill
salt and pepper
dill sprigs, to garnish

Method

1 Heat the olive oil in a large saucepan over medium heat. Add the onion and fennel and cook for 3–4 minutes, stirring occasionally, until the onion is just softened.

2 Add the potato, water, tomato juice, and bay leaf with a large pinch of salt. Reduce the heat, cover, and simmer for about 25 minutes, stirring once or twice, until the vegetables are soft.

3 Let the soup cool slightly, then remove and discard the bay leaf. Transfer to a food processor or blender and process until smooth, working in batches, if necessary. (If using a food processor, strain off the cooking liquid and reserve. Puree the soup solids with enough cooking liquid to moisten them, then combine with the reserved liquid.)

4 Return the soup to the saucepan and add the shrimp. Simmer gently for about 10 minutes to reheat the soup and let it absorb the shrimp flavor.

5 Stir in the tomatoes and dill. Taste and adjust the seasoning. Thin the soup with a little more tomato juice, if desired. Ladle into serving bowls, garnish with dill sprigs, and serve immediately.

38 GARLIC

Garlic has been used to treat disease and improve health for thousands of years. Its powerful compounds protect against heart disease, cancers, and digestive problems.

Garlic is a member of the same family as onions, leeks, and chives. Even a couple of cloves eaten regularly can benefit your health. It is rich in a variety of powerful sulfur compounds, such as allicin, which give it its pungent odor, and are the main source of its health benefits. Research has found that garlic can help reduce the risk of both heart disease and many types of cancer. High blood pressure, a common problem of aging, is kept under control by the sulfides, which help to dilate blood vessels. Garlic is also a powerful antibiotic, helps keep the digestion healthy, and appears to minimize stomach ulcers and prevent constipation. The diallyl sulfides help your body to absorb iron more easily—and so boost your energy levels. Garlic eaten in a reasonable quantity is also a good source of vitamin C and selenium, both of which are antioxidants, and of potassium and calcium.

- Reduces the risk of high blood pressure, heart disease, and some cancers.
- Antibiotic and helps protect and regularize the digestive system.
- Helps us absorb the iron in our diet.

Practical tips:
Garlic lightly fried in oil or baked until just soft contains the highest levels of its beneficial compounds. After eating garlic, chew fresh parsley to reduce mouth odor. If you eat garlic regularly, however, the telltale odor disappears.

DID YOU KNOW?
Research shows that if you crush or chop garlic and let it stand for a few minutes before using it in a recipe, the protective effects of its allicin content will be at their highest.

MAJOR NUTRIENTS PER 2 GARLIC CLOVES

Calories	9
Protein	0.4 g
Total fat	Trace
Carbohydrate	2 g
Fiber	Trace
Vitamin C	2 mg
Calcium	11 mg
Potassium	24 mg
Selenium	1 mcg

Lemon and garlic spinach

SERVES 4 (**W**)(**B**)(**H**)(**S**)

¼ cup olive oil

2 garlic cloves, thinly sliced

1 pound spinach, torn
  or shredded

juice of ½ lemon

pepper

Method

1 Heat the olive oil in a large skillet over high heat. Add the garlic and spinach and cook, stirring continuously, until the spinach is soft. Be careful to avoid letting the spinach burn.

2 Remove from the heat, turn into a serving bowl, and sprinkle with lemon juice. Season with pepper. Mix well and serve either hot or at room temperature.

39

LETTUCE

Lettuce and salad greens that are bright or deep green, red, or purple, are rich in plant compounds that can prevent disease and enhance our health in midlife.

For your menopausal health, it pays to choose varieties with a deep color instead of the pale iceberg types. Darker lettuce contains much higher levels of useful vitamins, such as vitamin C, minerals, antioxidants, and other plant chemicals. The carotenes in lettuce help guard against heart disease and some cancers, while the red pigments anthocyanins in red and purple types are flavonoids that can help maintain the suppleness and firmness in skin by boosting the underlying collagen. Lettuce is low in calories, high in insoluble fiber, and low on the glycemic index. The chemical lactucin found in lettuce is a sedative, so eating it in the evening helps guard against insomnia and minimizes anxiety. Dark lettuce is also rich in the compounds lutein and zeaxanthin, which can help prevent deterioration in eyesight, and in folic acid, which helps maintain a healthy heart and arteries.

- Nutritious low-calorie food for dieters.
- Anthocyanins can improve skin collagen and suppleness.
- Mildly sedative.
- Antioxidants and folic acid protect heart and arterial health.

Practical tips:
Don't leave lettuce soaking in water to clean because the vitamin C content will leach into the water. Rinse quickly in cold water and dry in a salad spinner. Keep the leaves whole or tear at the last minute before eating because the cut surfaces will quickly spoil.

DID YOU KNOW?
Salad greens with a strong or bitter flavor tend to contain higher levels of plant chemicals than mild ones.

MAJOR NUTRIENTS PER 2 CUPS CHOPPED (3½ oz.) DARK LETTUCE

Calories	17
Protein	1.2 g
Total fat	Trace
Carbohydrate	3.2 g
Fiber	2.1 g
Vitamin C	4 mg
Folic acid	136 mcg
Potassium	247 mg
Calcium	33 mg
Iron	1 mg
Beta-carotene	5,226 mcg
Lutein/Zeaxanthin	1,850 mcg

Peas with lettuce, shallots, and mint

SERES 6 (W) (B) (H) (M)

3½ cups shelled fresh peas

2 shallots, thinly sliced

1 garlic clove, finely chopped

8 romaine lettuce leaves, shredded

3 fresh mint sprigs, plus extra
*   to garnish*

1 teaspoon sugar

2 tablespoons butter or
*   sunflower oil*

salt and pepper

Method

1 Bring a saucepan of water to a boil. Line a steamer with
   dampened wax paper.

2 Put the peas into the steamer and add the shallots, garlic, lettuce,
   and mint sprigs. Sprinkle with the sugar and dot with the butter.
   Season with salt and pepper.

3 Cover the steamer with a tight-fitting lid and set the steamer over
   the pan of boiling water. Steam for about 4–5 minutes, until the
   peas are tender.

4 Remove and discard the mint sprigs. Transfer the vegetables to
   a serving dish, garnish with fresh mint sprigs and serve immediately.

40

BROCCOLI

Broccoli is packed with a huge range of nutrients and plant compounds that help protect and boost your health and body during and after menopause.

Broccoli is a member of the brassica family and comes in several forms, but it is the dark green and purple types that tend to contain the highest levels of nutrients, particularly carotenoids, which help to lower LDL cholesterol and protect against heart disease. Carotenoids also help improve memory and alleviate dry skin problems. Broccoli may help to minimize hot flashes and their effects, because it contains high levels of lignans, the plant compounds that have an estrogenic effect. It is also one of the best vegetable sources of calcium and vitamin K, both of which can protect against osteoporosis. Broccoli also contains a high level of sulforaphane, indoles, selenium, and immune-boosting vitamin C, all of which offer protection against breast cancer, a common disease during midlife and old age.

DID YOU KNOW?

The large broccoli heads most often for sale in the supermarkets are more correctly called calabrese, which is a particular variety of broccoli. The pale green varieties of the vegetable contain fewer of the healthy plant chemicals.

MAJOR NUTRIENTS PER 1 CUP CHOPPED (3½ oz.) BROCCOLI

Calories	34
Protein	2.8 g
Total fat	0.4 g
Carbohydrate	6.6 g
Fiber	2.6 g
Vitamin C	89 mg
Vitamin K	102 mcg
Selenium	2.5 mcg
Beta-carotene	361 mcg
Calcium	47 mg
Lutein/Zeaxanthin	1,403 mcg

- Contains compounds and nutrients that offer strong protection against breast cancer and heart disease.
- Estrogenic effect that helps minimize hot flashes.
- Low in calories and high in fiber, so a useful aid to weight control.
- Calcium and vitamin K helps build and protect bones.

Practical tips:

You can use either fresh or frozen broccoli; they contain equal amounts of nutrients and chemicals. Cook by lightly steaming or stir-frying to get the most vitamin C and antioxidants. The leaves and the stalks, which are full of fiber, are edible and good for you.

Broccoli hash with poached eggs

SERVES 4　Ⓑ Ⓜ Ⓢ

4 potatoes, such as red-skinned
　types or white rounders, peeled
　and cut into ½-inch cubes
2½ cups small broccoli florets
2 tablespoons sunflower oil
1 onion, finely chopped
1 large red bell pepper, seeded and
　finely diced
¼–½ teaspoon crushed red pepper
4 extra-large eggs
salt and pepper

Method

1　Cook the potatoes in lightly salted boiling water for 6 minutes.
　Drain well. Blanch or steam the broccoli for 3 minutes.

2　Heat the oil in a large skillet over high heat, add the onion and red
　bell pepper, and sauté for 2–3 minutes to soften. Add the potatoes
　and cook, turning occasionally, for 6–8 minutes, until tender. Stir in
　the broccoli and crushed red pepper, then let cook over low heat,
　turning the mixture occasionally, until golden brown. Season with
　salt and pepper.

3　Meanwhile, bring a large saucepan of water to just simmering point.
　Break the eggs into the water and poach gently for 3–4 minutes,
　until softly set.

4　Spoon the hash onto serving plates and top each portion with a
　poached egg.

41 GREEN BEANS

Green beans are easy to cook and go well with anything. They also contain nutrients and plant chemicals to help rejuvenate and nourish during menopause.

All types of green beans—French-style green beans, stringless beans, and Italian flat beans, for example—contain high levels of plant nutrients. They are especially rich in the carotenes lutein, beta-carotene, violaxanthin, and neoxanthin. Regular intake of these compounds helps protect us both from heart disease and cancers, and also protects the skin against sun damage. Green beans also contain lutein and zeaxanthin, which protect our eyesight as we age. The range of flavonoids they contain—quercetin, kaemferol, catechins, epicatechins, and procyanidins—help counteract free radical damage and so help ward off the signs of aging. Green beans can also protect bone density because of their calcium, vitamin K, and vitamin C content.

- Very high in carotenes, which offer protection from heart disease and cancers.
- Able to fight free radicals and ward off the signs of aging.
- Protect bones and boost brain capability.

Practical tips:
Choose fresh beans that snap easily, because soft beans will have lost much of their vitamin C and B content. Beans need only light steaming, and can also be used in stir-fries—the oil helps the absorption of carotenes into the body.

DID YOU KNOW?

Green beans come in a variety of colors other than green, including purple and yellow. The purple variety have a slightly higher flavonoid content than the green varieties; the yellow type slightly less.

MAJOR NUTRIENTS PER 1 CUP (3½ OZ.) GREEN BEANS

Calories	31
Protein	1.8 g
Total fat	0.2 g
Carbohydrate	7 g
Fiber	2.7 g
Vitamin C	12 mg
Folic acid	33 mcg
Vitamin K	14.5 mcg
Potassium	211 mg
Calcium	37 mg
Iron	1 mg
Beta-carotene	379 mcg
Lutein/Zeaxanthin	640 mcg

Green bean ratatouille

SERVES 4 (W)(B)(H)(S)

1 tablespoon olive oil

1 onion, chopped

2 garlic cloves, sliced

2 red bell peppers, seeded
   and chopped

2 zucchini, halved lengthwise
   and sliced

1½ cups 2-inch green bean pieces

2 cups green beans

1 (14½-ounce) can diced tomatoes

½ cup vegetable stock

2 tablespoons chopped fresh
   parsley

salt and pepper

¼ cup freshly grated Parmesan
   cheese, to serve (optional)

Method

1 Heat the olive oil in a saucepan over medium heat and sauté the
   onion and garlic for 2 minutes.

2 Stir in the remaining vegetables, then pour over the diced
   tomatoes and stock.

3 Season well with salt and pepper and bring to a boil. Reduce the
   heat and simmer, covered, for 25 minutes, until the vegetables are
   cooked but still firm to the bite.

4 Stir in the chopped parsley and serve sprinkled with the grated
   Parmesan cheese, if using.

42 SEAWEED

Seaweed in all its various forms is highly nutritious. It is rich in iodine for a healthy thyroid action, zinc for hormonal regulation, and calcium for strong bones.

There are several varieties of seaweed available, including dark green kelp (kombu), dark red dulse, green or purple nori (laver), and dark green or brown wakame. While the nutritional value of each varies somewhat, they are generally rich in iodine, a mineral that helps to boost the action of the thyroid gland, which makes hormones to regulate the body's metabolism. An underactive thyroid gland can cause weight gain and fatigue. Seaweeds also contain a broad spectrum of minerals, including zinc, which helps to control menopausal symptoms, such as hot flashes and night sweats, and can improve skin condition. Magnesium and calcium are needed for healthy bones, and a good dose of iron will give you energy and keep your memory in shape. The B vitamin folic acid in seaweed helps reduce levels of homocysteine in the blood and can reduce the risk of heart disease and stroke.

• Excellent source of iodine to support the body's metabolism.
• Range of minerals that alleviate menopausal symptoms.
• Rich in iron for memory and energy levels, and in calcium for healthy bones.
• High in folic acid, which keeps the arteries healthy.

Practical tips:
Fresh seaweed can be chopped and used in soups and stir-fries. Look for dried seaweed, such as wakame, laver, and sushi nori, which may need soaking to rehydrate, in Asian food stores.

DID YOU KNOW?

Most types of seaweed are high in sodium because the sea is very salty. Anyone on a low-sodium diet should, therefore, avoid sea vegetables.

MAJOR NUTRIENTS PER ⅔ CUP (1¾ OZ.) KELP

Calories	22
Protein	0.8 g
Total fat	0.3 g
Carbohydrate	4.8 g
Fiber	0.7 g
Calcium	84 mg
Iron	1.4 mg
Magnesium	61 mg
Potassium	45 mg
Zinc	0.6 mg
Iodine	1,037 mcg
Folic acid	90 mcg

Wakame, cucumber, and squid salad

SERVES 4　(**W**)(**H**)(**S**)

¾ ounce dried wakame

1 tablespoon peanut oil

1 garlic clove, finely chopped

1 red chile, seeded and finely
*   chopped*

4 tubes of squid, cut into thin rings

1 cucumber, halved, seeded,
*   and sliced*

1 cup bean sprouts

1 red bell pepper, seeded and
*   finely sliced*

small handful of cilantro leaves,
*   to garnish*

Dressing

3 tablespoons peanut oil

juice of ½ lime

1 teaspoon Thai fish sauce

½ teaspoon brown sugar

1¾-inch piece fresh ginger, grated

Method

1　Place the wakame in a bowl with enough cold water to cover and let soak for 4 minutes. Drain.

2　To make the dressing, beat together 3 tablespoons of the peanut oil with the lime juice, fish sauce, sugar, and ginger.

3　Heat the remaining oil in a saucepan. Sauté the garlic and chile for 1–2 minutes, add the squid, and stir-fry the squid for 2–3 minutes, until cooked. Remove from the pan and let cool slightly.

4　Toss the squid together with the cucumber, bean sprouts, bell pepper, wakame, and the dressing.

5　Transfer to a serving dish, garnish with cilantro leaves, and serve.

43

KALE

Deep green kale, a member of the brassica family, contains the highest levels of antioxidants of all vegetables and, as such, is an important food for our health.

Kale is one of the most nutritious green vegetables there is, being rich in a range of important nutrients. It contains as many as 45 different antioxidant compounds and, therefore, rates extremely highly on the ORAC scale. The flavonoid kaempferol, to name just one, can help to preserve bone density and ease menopausal depression and anxiety, while the indoles help lower LDL cholesterol. Kale tops the vegetable chart for calcium content, too, and this along with its vitamin K helps protect our bones during and after menopause. It is a good source of iron, for healthy blood and energy; of selenium, for a healthy immune system; and of magnesium, for a healthy heart. The vitamin E it contains also offers heart protection and may help to keep skin soft and supple. To complete the good news, kale is low in calories and low on the glycemic index.

- Rich in calcium and vitamin K for healthy bones.
- High vitamin C content encourages calcium absorption.
- Good source of iron, selenium, and magnesium.

Practical tips:
Kale is good steamed or stir-fried and the addition of a little oil in cooking helps the vitamin C to be absorbed. The outer, deepest green leaves contain the highest amount of antioxidant plant chemicals and iron. Wash kale before use under cold running water because the curly leaves may contain grit.

DID YOU KNOW?

Kale contains goitrogens, naturally occurring substances that can interfere with the functioning of the thyroid gland. People with thyroid problems may, therefore, be advised to avoid this vegetable.

MAJOR NUTRIENTS
PER 1½ CUPS (3½ OZ.) KALE

Calories	50
Protein	3.3 g
Total fat	0.7 g
Carbohydrate	10 g
Fiber	2 g
Vitamin C	120 mg
Folic acid	29 mcg
Vitamin E	1.7 mg
Potassium	447 mg
Calcium	135 mg
Iron	1.7 mg
Magnesium	34 mg
Selenium	0.9 mcg
Beta-carotene	9,226 mcg

Beans and greens stew

SERVES 4 (**W**) (**F**) (**B**) (**H**) (**M**)

1⅓ cups dried haricot or cannellini
beans, soaked overnight
1 tablespoon olive oil
2 onions, finely chopped
4 garlic cloves, finely chopped
1 celery stalk, thinly sliced
2 carrots, halved and thinly sliced
5 cups water
¼ teaspoon dried thyme
¼ teaspoon dried marjoram
1 bay leaf
4 ounces leafy greens,
such as kale, Swiss chard,
mustard, and spinach, washed
salt and pepper

Method

1 Drain the beans, put in a saucepan, and add enough cold water to cover by 2 inches. Bring to a boil and boil for 10 minutes. Drain and rinse well.

2 Heat the olive oil in a large saucepan over medium heat. Add the onions and cook, covered, for 3–4 minutes, stirring occasionally, until the onions are just softened. Add the garlic, celery, and carrots, and continue cooking for 2 minutes.

3 Add the water, drained beans, thyme, marjoram, and bay leaf. When the mixture begins to bubble, reduce the heat to low. Cover and simmer gently, stirring occasionally, for about 1¼ hours, until the beans are tender; the cooking time will vary depending on the type of bean. Season with salt and pepper.

4 Let the soup cool slightly, then remove and discard the bay leaf. Transfer 2 cups to a food processor or blender. Process until smooth, then return it to the stew and mix together.

5 Cut the greens crosswise into thin ribbons, keeping tender leaves, such as spinach, separate. Add the thicker leaves and cook gently, uncovered, for 10 minutes. Stir in any remaining greens and continue cooking for 5–10 minutes, until all the greens are tender. Serve immediately.

44 WATERCRESS

Although watercress is usually eaten in small quantities, the leaves still contain enough nutrients to make an important contribution to the midlife diet.

A serving of deep green, fresh watercress leaves provides good amounts of vitamins C and K, potassium, and calcium—a fantastic combination when it comes to bone strength and density, and to help prevent osteoporosis. The leaves are also a great source of carotenes, including lutein for eye health, and are rich in a variety of plant chemicals, such as phenylethyl isothiocyanate, which can help minimize the risk of midlife cancers. Watercress is also said to detoxify the liver and cleanse the blood, because it contains benzyl oil, which is a powerful antibiotic. It helps protect the skin from burning in the sun, too, and from dryness and wrinkles because of its vitamin C and beta-carotene content. Its use in traditional medicine is as a diuretic, appetite stimulant, and anti-depressant.

- Provides a combination of nutrients for bone health and strength.
- Carotene content helps protect against cancers.
- Strong protection for the skin against sun damage and the signs of aging.
- Low in calories.

Practical tips:
Wash and shake to remove excess water. Although usually eaten raw as a salad, watercress can be made into a tasty soup with potatoes and onion and none of the vitamins and plant chemicals will be lost. Add watercress to chicory leaves and orange slices drizzled with oil for a palate-cleansing, nutrient-rich salad.

DID YOU KNOW?

You should not pick watercress from natural sources, such as streams; they may carry parasites and bacteria that can cause intestinal infections.

MAJOR NUTRIENTS PER 10 (1 oz.) WATERCRESS SPRIGS

Calories	3
Protein	0.6 g
Total fat	Trace
Carbohydrate	0.3 g
Fiber	Trace
Vitamin C	11 mg
Vitamin K	62 mcg
Potassium	83 mg
Calcium	30 mg
Beta-carotene	705 mcg
Lutein/Zeaxanthin	1,442 mcg

Watercress and chicken stir-fry

SERVES 4   (W) (H) (B) (M) (F)

1 tablespoon olive oil
2 large skinless, boneless chicken
*   breasts, cut into strips*
1 tablespoon honey
6 scallions, sliced
2 red bell peppers, seeded
*   and sliced*
3 cups snow peas
3 cups halved cremini mushrooms
2½ cups coarsely chopped
*   watercress*
1 tablespoon light soy sauce
1 tablespoon hoisin sauce
3 tablespoons cashew nuts
freshly cooked brown rice or
*   noodles, to serve*

Method

1 Heat the olive oil in a wok or deep skillet and add the chicken and 2 teaspoons of the honey. Brown the chicken, then remove with a slotted spoon and reserve.

2 Add the scallions, red bell peppers, snow peas, and mushrooms with the remaining honey. Stir-fry over high heat for 2–3 minutes.

3 Return the chicken to the wok with the watercress, soy sauce, hoisin sauce, and cashew nuts. Cook for another 4–5 minutes.

4 Divide among four serving plates and serve immediately, accompanied by freshly cooked brown rice or noodles.

45 CUCUMBER

Cucumbers belong to the family that includes melon. Like melons, cucumbers are refreshing, hydrating, and a good source of nutrients of benefit to the skin.

There is some evidence that cucumber can help to build and maintain healthy connective tissue—ligaments and cartilage in our bodies—as we age. This is mainly because it is a good source of the mineral silica, which is an essential component of this tissue, as well as of bone and muscles. Both muscle mass and bone mass tend to diminish from the menopausal years onward. Cucumber also has a high water content, and helps to keep the skin hydrated and "plumped up" during menopause. It is also high in potassium, the mineral that helps regulate body fluid and acts as a diuretic, and is low in calories. Cucumber contains vitamin C and magnesium as well, which work together to look after the heart. Magnesium is also an important component of the bones and may help to prevent osteoporosis.

- Silica can help maintain connective tissue as we age.
- Diuretic and low in calories.
- Helps maintain a healthy heart and bones.

Practical tips:
Buy unwaxed—such as organic—cucumbers if you can, because then you will be able to eat the peel, which contains much of the fiber and many nutrients. It is almost always served raw: in salads, for dipping, or with yogurt as part of an Indian raita or Greek tzatziki. Although many recipes call for cucumber to be seeded, it is best to eat the seeds because they contain a lot of the nutrition.

DID YOU KNOW?

Gherkins are a type of cucumber, usually cultivated for pickling. They are small, with a slightly lower water content than regular cucumbers.

MAJOR NUTRIENTS PER ¾ CUP SLICED (3½ oz.) CUCUMBER

Calories	15
Protein	0.5 g
Total fat	Trace
Carbohydrate	3.5 g
Fiber	0.5 g
Vitamin C	3 mg
Vitamin K	16 mcg
Potassium	147 mg
Calcium	16 mg
Magnesium	13 mg
Iron	0.3 mg

Crunchy Thai salad

SERVES 4 (W) (H) (S)

1 cucumber, cut into thin strips
2 carrots, cut into thin strips
½ red bell pepper, seeded and cut
  into thin strips
1½ cups bean sprouts
1¼ cups sliced snow peas
2 tablespoons chopped fresh
  cilantro
⅓ cup salted peanuts, chopped,
  to serve

Dressing

1 tablespoon peanut oil
1 teaspoon sesame oil
½ teaspoon brown sugar
1 teaspoon Thai fish sauce
juice of 1 lime
1 red chile, seeded and
  finely sliced

Method

1 To make the dressing, beat together the peanut oil, sesame oil, sugar, fish sauce, and lime juice until the sugar has dissolved. Stir in the chile.

2 Place the cucumber, carrots, red bell pepper, bean sprouts, snow peas, and cilantro in a bowl and toss with the dressing.

3 Divide the salad among four serving bowls, sprinkle with chopped peanuts, and serve.

46 **TOMATOES**

Tomatoes are an ideal health food, containing a range of vitamins and compounds that can protect us against disease in midlife.

Raw tomatoes are rich in vitamin C, the antioxidant vitamin that reduces our risk of heart disease, boosts the work of the minerals that we eat in the service of our bones and blood, and improves the condition of our skin, gums, and eyes. They also contain vitamin E, magnesium, and folic acid for a healthy heart, and potassium, which works with sodium to control fluid retention. Tomatoes are a good source of iron, which is vital for energy, our brain, and a smooth-functioning memory. Tomatoes are an especially rich source of dietary carotene, including lycopene, which fights heart disease. Cooked, pureed, or partly dried tomatoes are even richer in this special antioxidant. All tomatoes are a good source of lipoic acid, which helps increase our energy levels and brain power.

- Rich in vitamins and antioxidants for a healthy heart.
- High in iron and lipoic acid for energy and brain power.
- Contain carotenes that help protect the skin and vitamin C, which boosts collagen, keeping skin firm and smooth.

Practical tips:
The redder and riper the tomato, the higher its carotene content. Vine-ripened tomatoes also contain more lycopene than ones that have been ripened after picking. Avoid peeling any tomatoes unless absolutely necessary, because the peel is richer in nutrients than the flesh.

DID YOU KNOW?

The central seed part of the tomato is high in salicylates, aspirin-like compounds to which some people are allergic and that can cause wheezing.

MAJOR NUTRIENTS PER 1 SMALL (3½ oz.) TOMATO

Calories	18
Protein	0.9 g
Total fat	0.2 g
Carbohydrate	3.9 g
Fiber	1.2 g
Vitamin C	12.7 mg
Potassium	237 mg
Lycopene	2,573 mcg
Lutein/Zeaxanthin	123 mcg

Hot tomato and basil salad

SERVES 6 （**W**）（**H**）（**S**）

1½ pounds cherry tomatoes

1 garlic clove, crushed

2 tablespoons drained and
  rinsed capers

1 teaspoon sugar

¼ cup olive oil

2 tablespoons torn fresh basil

Method

1 Preheat the oven to 400°F.

2 Stir together the tomatoes, garlic, capers, and sugar in a bowl and transfer to a roasting pan. Pour the oil over them and toss to coat.

3 Cook in the preheated oven for 10 minutes, until the tomatoes are hot.

4 Remove from the oven and transfer to a heatproof serving bowl. Scatter the basil over the tomatoes and serve immediately.

47 MUSHROOMS

Mushrooms form a useful part of a healthy diet. Even the cultivated types, such as cremini and portobello, are rich in disease-fighting nutrients.

Mushrooms are one of the best plant sources of the antioxidant mineral selenium, which has several benefits for menopausal women. It is important for healthy skin and hair and vital for proper thyroid action. It also has anti-inflammatory properties, which is why low selenium levels in the body are linked with a higher incidence of arthritis. Mushrooms are also a good source of choline, the vitamin-like substance that improves our blood cholesterol profile. Asian mushrooms—such as shiitake—tend to have higher levels of plant chemicals and beneficial nutrients than pale, cultivated white button mushrooms. They are particularly rich in the B vitamins, including niacin, which is vital to convert energy from food, and they also contain lentinan, the well-known immune booster and anticancer compound.

• Help maintain healthy skin, hair, and thyroid.
• Decrease the risk of hormone-dependent breast cancer.
• Able to fight other forms of cancer.

Practical tips:
Small, fresh mushrooms can be eaten raw, but they are also good stir-fried in olive oil or in sesame oil for use in Asian dishes. They are a good meat substitute in vegetarian dishes and enhance flavors when added to casseroles. To keep mushrooms fresh, store them in a paper bag in the refrigerator—plastic will make them turn rotten quickly.

DID YOU KNOW?
Mushrooms are fungi, which means they get the energy to grow from other plant materials, instead of through photosynthesis.

MAJOR NUTRIENTS PER 3½ oz. DARK-GILLED PORTOBELLO MUSHROOMS

Calories	22
Protein	2 g
Total fat	0.3 g
Carbohydrate	3.8 g
Fiber	1.3 g
Niacin	4.5 mg
Potassium	364 mg
Iron	0.3 mg
Selenium	18.6 mcg
Choline	21.2 mg

Mushrooms in tomato and onion sauce

SERVES 4   (W) (F) (H)

1 tablespoon sunflower oil
   or olive oil
1 onion, finely chopped
1 green chile, finely chopped
   (seeded if you prefer)
2 teaspoons garlic paste
1 teaspoon ground cumin
1 teaspoon ground coriander
½ teaspoon chili powder
4 cups thickly sliced closed-cup
   mushrooms
½ teaspoon salt
1 tablespoon tomato paste
3 tablespoons water
1 tablespoon snipped fresh chives,
   to garnish

Method

1 Heat the oil in a medium saucepan over medium heat. Add the onion and chile and cook, stirring frequently, for 5–6 minutes, until the onion is soft but not brown. Add the garlic paste and cook, stirring, for 2 minutes.

2 Add the cumin, coriander, and chili powder and cook, stirring, for 1 minute. Add the mushrooms, salt, and tomato paste, and stir until all the ingredients are thoroughly blended.

3 Sprinkle the water evenly over the mushrooms and reduce the heat to low. Cover and cook for 10 minutes, stirring halfway through. The sauce should have thickened, but if it appears runny, cook, uncovered, for 3–4 minutes, or until you achieve the desired consistency. Transfer to warm serving dishes, garnish with snipped chives, and serve immediately.

48

PEAS

Fresh or frozen, peas are rich in vitamins, including vitamin C for heart health, vitamin K for bone protection, and folic acid, which helps prevent stroke.

Peas are members of the legume family, which includes lentils, and as such contain more protein than many vegetables. This, coupled with their high fiber content, means that despite the sugar in them, which gives them their appealing sweet flavor, they are low on the glycemic index and useful both for dieters and diabetics. Their generous antioxidant content is also thought to help protect against diabetes. A good proportion of the fiber they contain is the soluble fiber pectin, which helps lower blood cholesterol and protects us against heart disease and stroke. Peas also contain phenols and flavonols that protect us from heart disease, and are high in the carotenes lutein and zeaxanthin, which protect eyesight as we age. The amino acid tryptophan that they contain helps the brain to produce serotonin, which has a calming effect and can help induce sleep.

- Excellent food for dieters and diabetics.
- Contain several heart-friendly nutrients and chemicals.
- Rich in carotenes that protect eyesight.
- Good source of tryptophan for relaxation and sleep.

Practical tips:

Choose young, fresh peas. Small peas and snow peas can be eaten raw, for maximum vitamin C, although their carotene content will not be so well absorbed. To cook, steam lightly or microwave; when boiled, the vitamin C content leaches into the water.

DID YOU KNOW?

Snow peas have a similar nutrient profile to shelled green peas, but have a slightly higher vitamin C content and slightly less protein.

MAJOR NUTRIENTS PER ⅔ CUP (3½ OZ.) SHELLED PEAS

Calories	81
Protein	5.4 g
Total fat	0.4 g
Carbohydrate	14.5 g
Fiber	5.1 g
Vitamin C	40 mg
Folic acid	65 mcg
Magnesium	33 mg
Potassium	244 mg
Iron	1.5mg
Lutein/Zeaxanthin	2,477 mcg

Pea fritters

SERVES 4   (W)(B)(H)(M)

2¼ cups whole-wheat flour
2¾ teaspoons baking powder
2 eggs, beaten
2 cups low-fat milk
2 cups frozen peas, defrosted
juice of ½ lemon
3 tablespoons chopped fresh mint
2 tablespoons olive oil
salt and pepper
fresh mint leaves, to garnish

Method

1 Place the flour and baking powder in a bowl and slowly beat in the eggs and milk to produce a thick batter.

2 Stir in the peas, lemon juice, and mint and season well with salt and pepper.

3 Heat the olive oil in a skillet and carefully place tablespoonfuls of the batter into the skillet. Cook the fritters for 2–3 minutes on each side, until golden. Remove and keep warm, repeating with the remaining batter.

4 Stack the fritters on a warm serving dish and serve immediately, garnished with fresh mint.

49

SPINACH

Spinach is rich in a range of protective nutrients, including vitamin K for bone strength, and vitamins C and E for skin and brain health during menopause.

Spinach contains many antioxidant flavonoid compounds that fight skin, breast, and other cancers. It is also extremely high in carotenes, particularly anticancer beta-carotene, and lutein and zeaxanthin, which protect our eyesight. It is an excellent source of vitamin K, which helps to boost bone strength and may help prevent osteoporosis, and vitamin C, another antioxidant, which can boost mood and aid the absorption of minerals in our bodies. The relatively high vitamin E content of spinach can improve dry skin conditions and vaginal dryness and may help protect the brain from a decline in mental powers as we age. Spinach is extremely heart friendly, too. One portion contains a whole day's recommended intake of folic acid, which helps minimize harmful homocysteine levels in the blood, and supports artery health. It also contains peptides, which can lower blood pressure. Meanwhile, the high fiber content helps keep your bowels regular.

- Flavonoid and carotene content protects against female cancers.
- Vitamin K encourages bone density.
- Contains carotenes, which are excellent for eye health.
- Rich in folic acid for heart disease prevention.

Practical tips:
Increase carotene absorption by eating the leaves with a little oil in a salad or stir-frying. To retain the most antioxidants, cook by steaming or stir-frying. Avoid yellowing leaves.

DID YOU KNOW?

Although spinach contains good amounts of iron and calcium, these are not well absorbed by the body because spinach contains oxalic acid, which hinders the absorption process. However, the high vitamin C content partly counteracts this effect.

MAJOR NUTRIENTS PER 3 cups (3½ oz.) SPINACH

Calories	23
Protein	2.9 g
Total fat	0.4 g
Carbohydrate	3.6 g
Fiber	2.2 g
Vitamin C	28 mg
Folic acid	194 mcg
Vitamin E	2 mg
Vitamin K	482 mcg
Potassium	558 mg
Magnesium	79 mg
Calcium	99 mg
Iron	2.7 mg
Beta-carotene	5,626 mcg
Lutein/Zeaxanthin	12,198 mcg

Seafood and spinach salad

SERVES 4   (W) (B) (H)

1 pound mussels, scrubbed and
    debearded
4 ounces shrimp, peeled
    and deveined
12 ounces scallops
1 pound baby spinach leaves
¼ cup water
3 scallions, finely sliced

Dressing

¼ cup extra virgin olive oil
2 tablespoons white wine vinegar
1 tablespoon lemon juice
1 tablespoon finely grated
    lemon rind
1 garlic clove, chopped
1 tablespoon grated fresh ginger
1 small red chile, seeded
    and diced
1 tablespoon chopped fresh
    cilantro
salt and pepper

Method

1 Discard any mussels with broken shells and any that refuse to close when tapped. Put the mussels into a large saucepan with a little water, bring to a boil, and cook over high heat for 4 minutes. Drain and reserve the liquid. Discard any mussels that remain closed. Return the reserved liquid to the pan and bring to a boil. Add the shrimp and scallops and cook for 3 minutes. Drain. Remove the mussels from their shells. Rinse the mussels, shrimp, and scallops in cold water, drain, and put them in a large bowl. Cool, cover with plastic wrap, and chill for 45 minutes.

2 Meanwhile, rinse the spinach leaves and transfer them to a saucepan with ¼ cup of water. Cook over high heat for 1 minute and transfer to a colander. Refresh under cold running water and drain.

3 To make the dressing, put all the ingredients into a small bowl and mix.

4 Arrange the spinach on serving dishes, then scatter half of the scallions over the top. Top with the mussels, shrimp, and scallops, then scatter the remaining scallions over them. Drizzle over the dressing and serve.

50 SQUASH

Orange-fleshed squashes are full of carotenes, powerful plant compounds that protect us from cancer and other diseases and help to keep skin in good condition.

Squashes are related to pumpkin, cucumber, and melon. The orange-flesh varieties of squash, such as butternut, contain the highest levels of beneficial carotenes. Butternut squash is one of our richest sources of beta-cryptoxanthin, a carotene that is linked with protection from cancer. Squash, in general, is one of our top three sources of lutein and zeaxanthin, the carotenes associated with good eyesight as we age. The other carotenes in the vegetable help reduce the inflammation associated with arthritis and arterial disease. Squash is also a good source of antioxidant vitamins C and E, both of which can lift the libido and keep our skin firm. Calcium, iron, and magnesium are all present in good amounts, too, keeping our bones strong, our energy up, and our brains working on full power.

- Carotenes help protect us from cancer.
- Rich in compounds that protect our eyesight as we age.
- Works to reduce inflammation and the symptoms of arthritis.
- Contains vitamins to boost libido and skin collagen.
- Contains minerals to encourage bone density.

Practical tips:
The carotenes in squash are better absorbed if you eat them with a little oil, so roast cubes in olive oil, or steam the flesh, then mash with oil. Squash will keep well in a cool, dry frost-free place for up to six months.

DID YOU KNOW?
The seeds that you scoop from the center of the squash are packed with nutrients and can be washed, dried, and eaten just as you would store-bought pumpkin seeds.

MAJOR NUTRIENTS PER 1 CUP DICED (5½ OZ.) BUTTERNUT SQUASH

Calories	68
Protein	1.5
Total fat	Trace
Carbohydrate	17.5 g
Fiber	3 g
Vitamin C	31 mg
Niacin	1.8 mg
Folic acid	41 mcg
Vitamin E	2.2 mg
Potassium	528 mg
Calcium	72 mg
Iron	1 mg
Magnesium	51 mg
Beta-carotene	6,339 mcg
Beta-cryptoxanthin	5,027 mcg

Butternut squash stir-fry

SERVES 4 (W) (H) (M) (S)

3 tablespoons peanut oil

2¼ pounds butternut squash,
    peeled and cubed

1 onion, sliced

2 garlic cloves, crushed

1 teaspoon coriander seeds

1 teaspoon cumin seeds

2 tablespoons chopped fresh
    cilantro, plus extra to garnish

⅔ cup coconut milk

½ cup water

¾ cup unsalted cashew nuts

lime wedges, to serve

Method

1 Heat the oil in a large preheated wok. Add the squash, onion, and
   garlic to the wok and stir-fry for 5 minutes.

2 Stir in the coriander seeds, cumin seeds, and chopped cilantro and
   stir-fry for 1 minute.

3 Add the coconut milk and water to the wok and bring to a boil.
   Cover the wok and let simmer for 10–15 minutes, or until the
   squash is tender.

4 Add the cashew nuts and stir to combine thoroughly.

5 Divide among four serving bowls and garnish with chopped cilantro.
   Serve with lime wedges for squeezing over.

BELL PEPPERS

51

Red and orange sweet peppers contain high levels of over thirty different carotenes, offering protection for the heart, skin, and against cancer.

Bell peppers come in a variety of colors, but the red, purple, and orange ones contain the highest levels of carotenes, which have been the subject of extensive research for their anticancer properties. Carotenes also have important benefits for heart and artery health, eye health, and skin protection. Peppers are rich in vitamins C and E, too, both important vitamins when it comes to heart protection, and which also help to keep our memory and skin in shape as we age. It is thought that when these vitamins are present with carotene, they act synergistically in our bodies, enhancing each other's action. Other plant compounds present in peppers include phenols and sterols that protect against cancer.

- One of the best sources of the antioxidant trio—carotenes, vitamin C, and vitamin E—which work together effectively in the body.
- Regular intake can protect our memory and skin.
- Contain several components that are strongly anticancer and protect us from artery disease.

Practical tips:
The carotene is absorbed more easily if bell peppers are cooked or eaten with a little oil. Stir-fry slices with red onions for a side dish or seed and halve, brush with oil, and roast. Choose the ripest peppers possible for maximum carotene and also vitamin C content. Peppers can be seeded, sliced, bagged, and frozen.

DID YOU KNOW?
Peppers are closely related to chillies. Sweet paprika is made from sweet peppers, while hot paprika is made from chillies.

MAJOR NUTRIENTS
PER ⅔ CUP CHOPPED (3½ oz.) RED PEPPER

Calories	31
Protein	1g
Total fat	0.3 g
Carbohydrate	6 g
Fiber	2 g
Vitamin C	128 mg
Folic acid	46 mcg
Niacin	0.98 mg
Vitamin B6	0.3 mg
Vitamin E	1.6 mg
Potassium	211 mg
Iron	0.4 mg
Beta-carotene	1,624 mcg
Beta-cryptoxanthin	490 mcg
Lutein/Zeaxanthin	51 mcg

Chicken pepperonata

SERVES 4 (W)(F)(B)(H)(M)(S)

8 skinless chicken thighs
2 tablespoons whole-wheat flour
2 tablespoons olive oil
1 small onion, thinly sliced
1 garlic clove, crushed
1 large red bell pepper, yellow bell
* pepper, and green bell pepper,*
* seeded and thinly sliced*
1 (14½-ounce) can diced tomatoes
1 tablespoon chopped fresh
* oregano, plus extra to garnish*
salt and pepper
crusty whole-wheat bread, to serve

Method

1 Toss the chicken thighs in the flour, shaking off the excess. Heat the oil in a large skillet over high heat and cook the chicken quickly until sealed and lightly browned, then remove from the skillet.

2 Add the onion to the skillet and gently cook until soft. Add the garlic, bell peppers, tomatoes, and oregano. Bring to a boil, stirring.

3 Arrange the chicken over the vegetables, season well with salt and pepper, and cover the skillet tightly and simmer for 20–25 minutes. Cook until the chicken is tender and the juices run clear when the tip of a sharp knife is inserted into the thickest part of the meat.

4 Taste and adjust the seasoning, adding salt and pepper, if needed. Garnish with oregano and serve with crusty whole-wheat bread.

52 ONIONS

All types of onion are excellent to eat during menopause because they contain a range of compounds that fight disease and nutrients to improve skin condition.

The pungent odor and flavor of onions comes from the sulfide compounds they contain, which help prevent the most common cancers of midlife, including breast and ovarian cancer. Onions—particularly red onions—also contain numerous flavonoids, such as quercetin, which helps to retain the collagen in the skin that can diminish rapidly around the menopausal years, and tannins, which protect against heart disease, high cholesterol, and cancer. In addition, onions are rich in chromium, a trace mineral that helps our cells respond to insulin and can protect us from type 2 diabetes. Onions are a surprisingly good source of vitamin C, which also boosts collagen, as well as brain function, bone health, and skin. All onions have an anti-inflammatory action and can strengthen the immune system.

- Compound- and nutrient-rich, providing a boost to collagen and skin condition.
- Rich in sulfides that protect against cancer and heart-protective nutrients.
- Can help regulate insulin response, protecting us from diabetes.

Practical tips:
Firm onions will store well in a cool but dry place for several weeks. The flavonoids in onion are mainly concentrated in the outer layers so peel off as little as necessary. Don't overbrown onions when sautéing because this destroys the beneficial sulfide compounds.

DID YOU KNOW?

Research has found that for maximum health benefits, you need to eat a portion of onion—about 3½ ounces, or 1 medium onion—most days; it is easily obtained, for example, from a serving of most casseroles or a small bowl of onion soup.

MAJOR NUTRIENTS PER AVERAGE-SIZE ONION

Calories	63
Protein	1.4 g
Total fat	Trace
Carbohydrate	15 g
Fiber	2.1 g
Vitamin C	9.6 mg
Folic acid	29 mcg
Calcium	33 mg
Potassium	216 mg
Magnesium	28 mg
Selenium	0.8 mcg
Chromium	24 mcg

French onion soup with Parmesan chips

SERVES 4 (W) (B) (H) (S)

1½ tablespoons butter

2 tablespoons olive oil

1 teaspoon dark brown sugar

4 large onions, thinly sliced

3 garlic cloves, thinly sliced

2 sprigs chopped fresh thyme,
*   plus extra to garnish*

1 tablespoon cognac

4 cups beef stock

½ cup white wine

1 cup grated Parmesan cheese

Method

1 Heat the butter and olive oil in a skillet over high heat and stir in the sugar, onions, garlic, and thyme. Cook, stirring occasionally, until the onions start to caramelize, turning the bottom of the skillet golden brown. Reduce the heat and continue to cook for about 20 minutes, stirring from time to time.

2 Pour in the cognac and let it be absorbed by the onions before pouring in the stock and white wine. Let simmer and cook gently for 1 hour. Meanwhile, preheat the oven to 400°F and line a baking sheet with parchment paper.

3 Arrange the Parmesan cheese on the baking sheet in mounds of 2 tablespoons each, then cook in the preheated oven for 4–5 minutes, until melted. Remove from the oven, let cool slightly, then peel off the paper.

4 Divide the soup among four serving bowls and garnish with thyme sprigs. Serve with the Parmesan chips on the side.

3

Meat, Fish, and Dairy

It is easy to overlook the importance of high-protein foods, such as red meat, poultry, white and oily fish, shellfish, and dairy products within your diet—however, nutritionally, each has real benefits in helping to reduce menopausal symptoms and ensure general good health. This group of foods provides nutrients that can be hard to get elsewhere.

(**W**) Ideal for weight control

(**F**) High in fiber

(**B**) Protects and strengthens bones

(**H**) Heart health

(**M**) Mood booster

(**S**) Improves skin condition

53 CHICKEN

Skinless chicken breast is one of the best animal sources of high-quality protein that you can choose. It is low in fat and calories, but rich in a range of nutrients.

Skinless chicken is a low-fat source of protein, especially the light breast meat. Of the fat chicken does contain, almost half is monounsaturated and only one-quarter is saturated. Chicken meat is high in niacin (vitamin B3) and choline, which help to lower blood cholesterol and improve your total blood fats profile, making it a heart-friendly choice. Like all animal protein, it is termed "high-quality protein" because it contains all the nine essential amino acids that our bodies need, unlike most plant sources. Adequate protein is vital during our middle years to maintain muscle mass, which tends to diminish at this time. A reduction in muscle is one of the main reasons why the metabolic rate slows down as we age, and weight gain follows. Chicken is rich in selenium, which as well as lifting mood is also a powerful anticancer mineral, minimizing our risk of cancers that mainly occur in mid- and later life.

- Low-fat source of high-quality protein that helps us maintain muscle mass and metabolic rate.
- Contains several nutrients of benefit to heart health.
- Selenium improves mood and helps prevent cancers.

Practical tips:
The healthiest ways to cook chicken are poaching, steaming, and in casseroles. Broiling and grilling produces carcinogens that, if eaten too frequently, are linked with cancers. Cook poultry all the way through—any pink meat can cause food poisoning.

DID YOU KNOW?

Organic chickens and chickens allowed to roam freely and find their own food contain more of the beneficial polyunsaturated fats and fewer of the saturates.

MAJOR NUTRIENTS PER 3½ oz. LEAN CHICKEN BREAST

Calories	114
Protein	21 g
Total fat	2.6 g
Niacin	10.4 mg
Vitamin B12	0.2 mg
Vitamin B6	0.7 mg
Vitamin D	5 IU
Choline	73 mg
Calcium	5 mg
Iron	0.4 mg
Magnesium	26 mg
Potassium	370 mg
Zinc	0.6 mg
Selenium	32 mcg
Phosphorous	210 mg

Chicken and pine nuts with couscous

SERVES 1   (**W**)(**F**)(**B**)(**H**)(**M**)(**S**)

1–2 saffron strands

¼ cup couscous

2 teaspoons golden raisins

½ cup boiling hot chicken
   or vegetable stock

1 chicken breast fillet, about
   4 ounces, cut into 8 strips

¼ cup corn kernels

1 teaspoon pine nuts

10 cherry tomatoes, cut into
   quarters

2 scallions, chopped

fresh cilantro leaves, to garnish

Dressing

1 teaspoon finely chopped fresh
   cilantro leaves

juice of ½ lemon

1 teaspoon olive oil

Method

1 Put the saffron, couscous, and golden raisins in a heatproof bowl and pour over the hot stock. Stir once and let stand for 15 minutes.

2 Meanwhile, beat together the dressing ingredients.

3 Heat a nonstick skillet over high heat, then brown the chicken strips on all sides for about 4 minutes. Reduce the heat to medium, add the corn kernels and pine nuts, and cook for another 2 minutes, stirring once or twice. Remove the chicken from the skillet and set aside.

4 Fluff up the couscous with a fork and add to the skillet with the tomatoes, dressing, and scallions. Heat for 1 minute, or until warmed through, stirring gently.

5 Spoon onto a serving plate, then top with the chicken strips and garnish with cilantro leaves.

54 BEEF

Lean beef is a fine source of top-quality protein. It also offers a range of minerals and vitamins that give us more energy and protect our health during menopause.

Red meat is avoided by many health-conscious women who believe, wrongly, that it is a high saturated fat item that is "bad for you." In fact, lean beef—especially if it is fed on grass—is lower in total fat and saturates than many other foods and other meats, and it is safe to eat 1–2 small servings a week. Lean beef is also low in calories and is high in protein, and a small serving will keep you feeling full for a long time. A high-protein diet is known to speed up the metabolic rate, so in several ways lean beef is an ideal food for women watching their weight. It is also one of the best sources of a range of the B vitamins that help to protect the heart, arteries, and nervous system. It contains various minerals, too, including iron, which is useful in menopause to maintain energy levels and brain power; zinc, which can lift a flagging libido, minimize hot flashes, and improve skin condition; and selenium, which helps beat depression and low mood.

- High-protein food that is ideal for weight control.
- Rich in the B vitamins for general menopausal health.
- Helps to maintain energy, heighten libido, and beat depression and hot flashes.

DID YOU KNOW?

Grass-fed beef contains a fat called conjugated linoleic acid (CLA), which is thought to lower cholesterol, keep the arteries clean, and may even speed up the metabolic rate.

MAJOR NUTRIENTS PER 3½ oz. LEAN BEEF

Calories	117
Protein	23 g
Total fat	2.7 g
Niacin	6.7 mg
Vitamin B12	1.3 mg
Vitamin B6	0.6 mg
Choline	65 mg
Calcium	9 mg
Iron	1.8 mg
Magnesium	23 mg
Potassium	342 mg
Zinc	3.6 mg
Selenium	21 mcg
Phosphorous	212 mg

Practical tips:
Choose lean cuts and remove any visible fat before cooking. Try marinating cubes of beef in a dressing and threading onto kabob skewers with vegetables—broil or grill lightly.

Hot sesame beef

SERVES 4   (**W**) (**F**) (**H**)

1 pound tenderloin steak,
   cut into thin strips
1½ tablespoons sesame seeds
½ cup beef stock
2 tablespoons light soy sauce
2 tablespoons grated fresh ginger
2 garlic cloves, finely chopped
1 teaspoon cornstarch
½ teaspoon crushed red pepper
3 tablespoons sesame oil
1 large head of broccoli,
   cut into florets
1 orange bell pepper, thinly sliced
1 red chile, seeded and finely sliced
1 tablespoon chili oil (optional)
1 tablespoon chopped fresh
   cilantro, to garnish
cooked wild rice, to serve

Method

1   Mix the beef strips with 1 tablespoon of the sesame seeds in a small bowl. In a separate bowl, beat together the beef stock, soy sauce, ginger, garlic, cornstarch, and crushed red pepper.

2   Heat 1 tablespoon of the sesame oil in a large skillet or wok. Stir-fry the beef strips for 2–3 minutes. Remove and set aside.

3   Discard any remaining oil in the skillet, then wipe with paper towels to remove any stray sesame seeds. Heat the remaining oil, add the broccoli, orange bell pepper, chile, and chili oil (if using) and stir-fry for 2–3 minutes. Stir in the beef stock mixture, cover, and simmer for 2 minutes.

4   Return the beef to the skillet and simmer until the juices thicken, stirring occasionally. Cook for another 1–2 minutes.

5   Sprinkle with the remaining sesame seeds. Serve over cooked wild rice garnished with fresh cilantro.

55

PORK

Pork has a reputation as a high-calorie, fatty food choice, but if you choose the right cut, it is a good lean source of protein and contains many key nutrients.

MAJOR NUTRIENTS PER 3½ oz. LEAN PORK TENDERLOIN

Calories	109
Protein	21 g
Total fat	2.2 g
Niacin	6.7 mg
Vitamin B12	0.5 mg
Vitamin B6	0.8 mg
Vitamin D	8 IU
Choline	80 mg
Calcium	5 mg
Iron	1 mg
Magnesium	27 mg
Potassium	399 mg
Zinc	1.9 mg
Selenium	31 mcg
Phosphorous	247 mg

If you want top-quality lean protein, buy pork tenderloin or cuts from the leg. They contain even less fat than lean beef, chicken, or turkey, and there is marginally more healthy monounsaturated fat in the meat than there is saturated. Lean pork is rich in choline and the B vitamins, all of which help to protect the arteries from cholesterol damage and, therefore, prevent cardiovascular diseases. Pork is high in potassium, the mineral that acts as a natural diuretic, reducing fluid retention and helping control high blood pressure. Eating pork is an excellent way to get your zinc, as well. This is the mineral that can help regulate your hormones and minimize menopausal symptoms, such as hot flashes and night sweats. There's iron, too, half of which is heme iron—the type that is most easily absorbed.

- Very good source of lean, high-quality protein.
- High in potassium to control high blood pressure.
- Contains several heart-protective nutrients.
- Zinc regulates hormones, and heme iron gives healthy blood.

Practical tips:
Pork tenderloin or leg can be cubed and used for kabobs, or try cooking like steak. Thinly sliced, pork makes a good addition to stir-fries. Lean pork freezes well and will keep for a year. Note that you should consume no more than 1 pound a week of red meat; a high intake is linked with an increased risk of heart disease.

Pork with cinnamon

SERVES 4 (W)(F)(H)(M)

1 pound pork tenderloin, diced
1 tablespoon vegetable oil
1 large onion, sliced
2-inch piece fresh ginger, finely
    chopped
4 garlic cloves, finely chopped
1 cinnamon stick
6 green cardamom pods
6 whole cloves
2 bay leaves
¾ cup water
salt

Marinade

1 teaspoon ground coriander
1 teaspoon ground cumin
1 teaspoon chili powder
⅔ cup plain yogurt

Method

1 To make the marinade, mix together the coriander, cumin, chili
   powder, and yogurt in a small bowl. Place the pork in a large,
   shallow nonmetallic dish and add the marinade, turning well
   to coat. Cover with plastic wrap and let marinate in the refrigerator
   for 30 minutes.

2 Heat the oil in a large, heavy saucepan. Cook the onion over low
   heat, stirring occasionally, for 5 minutes, or until soft. Add the
   ginger, garlic, cinnamon stick, cardamom pods, cloves, and bay
   leaves and cook, stirring continuously, for 2 minutes, or until the
   spices give off their aroma. Add the meat with its marinade and the
   water, and season with salt. Bring to a boil, reduce the heat, cover,
   and simmer for 30 minutes. Remove and discard the bay leaves.

3 Transfer the meat mixture to a preheated wok or large, heavy skillet
   and cook over low heat, stirring continuously, until dry and tender. If
   necessary, occasionally sprinkle with a little water to prevent it from
   sticking to the wok. Serve immediately.

56 TURKEY

Without the skin, turkey is a low-fat poultry with a good range of nutrients, including an amino acid that can improve depression and aid sleep.

Turkey is a high-protein alternative to chicken, with a rich, deep flavor. If you choose the dark meat (skin removed) instead of the pale breast, you will be getting even more of its beneficial nutrients. This dark meat contains a considerable amount more iron than chicken or pork. Iron is vital during perimenopause to help replace red blood cells and during menopause to help the brain work efficiently, and support memory and concentration. Turkey is also one of the meats highest in zinc, the antioxidant mineral that regulates female hormones and may alleviate hot flashes and mood swings. Zinc is also involved in keeping the skin healthy. Like several other sources of animal protein, turkey is a good source of tryptophan, the amino acid believed to combat depression and aid sleep. Tryptophan works by being converted in the brain to the chemical serotonin, which has a calming effect, and melatonin, the hormone that regulates sleep patterns.

- Low-fat, good-quality protein source, which is rich in nutrients.
- High iron and zinc content.
- Contains tryptophan, which alters the brain chemistry to promote good mood and better sleep patterns.

Practical tips:
Turkey can be used instead of pork or chicken in almost any recipe. You don't have to buy a whole turkey. Try using leg cuts or turkey pieces in a stir-fry.

DID YOU KNOW?
Turkeys are native to Mexico and were first brought to Europe by Christopher Columbus in 1519.

MAJOR NUTRIENTS PER 3½ oz. DARK TURKEY MEAT, NO SKIN

Calories	111
Protein	20.5 g
Total fat	2.7 g
Niacin	3 mg
Vitamin B12	0.4 mg
Vitamin B6	0.4 mg
Calcium	13 mg
Iron	1.7 mg
Magnesium	22 mg
Potassium	244 mg
Zinc	2.7 mg
Selenium	28.6 mcg
Phosphorous	171 mg

Turkey kabobs with cilantro pesto

SERVES 4 (**W**) (**F**) (**H**) (**M**) (**S**)

4 turkey steaks, about 4 ounces
    each, cut into 2-inch cubes
2 zucchini, thickly sliced
1 red and 1 yellow bell pepper,
    seeded and cut into
    2-inch cubes
8 cherry tomatoes
8 pearl onions, peeled

Marinade

⅓ cup olive oil
3 tablespoons dry white wine
1 teaspoon green peppercorns,
    crushed
2 tablespoons chopped fresh
    cilantro
salt

Cilantro pesto

1⅓ cups fresh cilantro leaves
¼ cup fresh parsley leaves
1 garlic clove
½ cup pine nuts
¼ cup grated Parmesan cheese
⅓ cup extra virgin olive oil
juice of 1 lemon

Method

1 Place the turkey in a large, glass bowl. To make the marinade, mix together the olive oil, wine, peppercorns, and cilantro in a small bowl and season with salt. Pour the mixture over the turkey and toss until the turkey is thoroughly coated. Cover with plastic wrap and let marinate in the refrigerator for 2 hours.

2 To make the cilantro pesto, put the cilantro and parsley into a food processor or blender and process until finely chopped. Add the garlic and pine nuts and process until chopped. Add the Parmesan cheese, olive oil, and lemon juice and process briefly to mix. Transfer to a bowl, cover, and let chill in the refrigerator until required.

3 If using wooden skewers, soak them in water for 30 minutes to prevent them from burning. Preheat a broiler to medium–hot. Drain the turkey, reserving the marinade. Thread the turkey, zucchini slices, bell pepper pieces, tomatoes, and onions alternately onto 8 metal or presoaked wooden skewers. Cook under the preheated broiler, turning and brushing often with the marinade, for 10 minutes, or until cooked through. Serve immediately with the cilantro pesto.

57

SALMON

Salmon is an excellent source of omega-3 fatty acids, which have several beneficial properties. Salmon is also rich in a range of vitamins and minerals.

MAJOR NUTRIENTS PER 3½ oz. FARMED SALMON FILLET

Calories	183
Protein	19.9 g
Total fat	10.8 g
EPA	0.618 g
DHA	1.293 g
Niacin	7.5 g
Vitamin B6	0.6 mg
Vitamin B12	2.8 mcg
Folic acid	26 mcg
Vitamin E	1.9 mg
Potassium	362 mg
Selenium	36.5 mcg
Magnesium	28 mg
Zinc	0.4 mg

Salmon is our major source of the fish oils eicosapentaenoic acid (EPA) and docosahexaeonic acid (DHA), types of omega-3 fatty acids that provide many health benefits during menopause and in old age. Benefits include protection against heart disease and stroke, because they can reduce the risk of blood clots, and against high blood pressure and high blood cholesterol. They may also help prevent Alzheimer's disease. The omega-3s are valuable, too, in combating depression, dry skin, and low libido. Plus, several research studies show a link between these fatty acids and brain function and memory. Omega-3 fatty acids are even anti-inflammatory, so they can help minimize the pain of arthritis and reduce its severity. Salmon is also a good source of selenium, which protects against cancer and can help lift mood; the B vitamins to ease anxiety and nervousness; magnesium, which helps to maintain strong bones; and vitamin E for heart and skin health.

• Protection against cardiovascular disease, arthritis, and cancer.
• Helps fight depression, anxiety, and low libido.
• Helps to keep bones and skin in good condition.

Practical tips:
Cook salmon lightly—steaming or poaching is ideal. Overcooking, particularly by broiling, can oxidize the essential fats and produce free radicals that damage body cells and contribute to aging. Frozen salmon retains the beneficial oils, vitamins, and minerals.

Roasted salmon with lemon and herbs

SERVES 4 (W) (B) (H) (M) (S)

⅓ cup extra virgin olive oil

1 onion, sliced

1 leek, sliced

juice of ½ lemon

2 tablespoons chopped fresh
   parsley

2 tablespoons chopped fresh dill

1 pound salmon fillets

salt and pepper

freshly cooked baby spinach leaves
   and lemon wedges, to serve

Method

1 Preheat the oven to 400°F. Heat 1 tablespoon of the oil in a skillet over medium heat. Add the onion and leek and cook, stirring, for about 4 minutes, until slightly soft.

2 Meanwhile, put the remaining oil in a small bowl with the lemon juice and herbs and season with salt and pepper. Stir together well. Rinse the fish under cold running water, then pat dry with paper towels. Arrange the fish in a shallow, ovenproof baking dish.

3 Remove the skillet from the heat and spread the onion and leek over the fish. Pour the oil mixture over the top, ensuring that everything is well coated. Roast in the center of the preheated oven for about 10 minutes, or until the fish is cooked through.

4 Arrange the cooked spinach on serving plates. Remove the fish and vegetables from the oven and arrange on top of the spinach. Serve immediately, accompanied by lemon wedges.

58 CRAB

Crab is one of the best shellfish to choose during menopause. It contains a range of nutrients to safeguard health and protect us from the diseases of midlife.

Crabmeat contains several nutrients and chemicals that can improve mood. Its B vitamins help calm anxiety and mood swings, while the selenium it contains is also thought to lift depression (and is also a strong protector against cancers). Crab is rich in tryptophan, an amino acid that converts to serotonin—a calming chemical—in the brain. This aids restful sleep and reduces anxiety and depression. The high zinc content is able to regulate female hormones and may reduce hot flashes and night sweats, while vitamin E, zinc, and selenium together form a powerful trio that improves dry skin conditions and libido. Crabmeat is high in protein, which speeds up the metabolic rate and suppresses hunger for hours after you eat. It is also low in fat and calories, so is an ideal food for women watching their weight.

- Contains a range of nutrients to improve mood and sleep and calm anxiety.
- Zinc regulates hormones and may reduce menopausal symptoms, such as hot flashes.
- Good choice for weight control.

Practical tips:

Frozen crabmeat is virtually as good nutritionally as fresh crab, while canned crab may be high in sodium. Crab is a rich meat; try it with green salad and lemon juice. One whole average crab will yield no more than a single portion, about 3½ ounces.

DID YOU KNOW?

Crabs have to cast their shell—or "molt"—every so often in order to increase in size. If a crab is caught when it has just molted, it has a new, soft shell. These soft shell crabs are thought by many to have tastier flesh. Nutritionally, they are no different.

MAJOR NUTRIENTS PER 3½ oz. CRAB, DARK AND LIGHT MEAT

Calories	90
Protein	18.5 g
Total fat	4.3 g
Niacin	2.5 mg
Vitamin B12	9 mcg
Folic acid	44 mcg
Vitamin E	1.8 mg
Selenium	34.5 mcg
Magnesium	49 mg
Potassium	173 mg
Zinc	2.8 mg

Crab cakes

MAKES 8 (W) (M)

1-inch piece fresh ginger, grated

2 red chiles, seeded and
     finely diced

grated rind of 1 lemon

10 ounces white crabmeat

3 scallions, finely sliced

1 tablespoon chopped
     fresh cilantro

2 extra-large eggs

2 cups fresh white bread crumbs

2 tablespoons all-purpose flour

2 tablespoons olive oil

salad greens, to serve

Method

1 In a large bowl, mix together the ginger, chiles, lemon rind, crabmeat, scallions, cilantro, one egg, and half the bread crumbs. Shape the mixture into 8 patty-shape cakes.

2 Beat the remaining egg and place in a shallow dish. Place the remaining bread crumbs and the flour in two other, separate shallow dishes.

3 Dip each cake first in flour, then into the egg, and finally into the bread crumbs to coat. Chill the coated cakes in the refrigerator for 20 minutes.

4 Heat the oil in a skillet and cook the cakes for 4–5 minutes on each side, or until golden and crisp all over. Serve with salad greens.

59

TUNA

Fresh tuna is a good source of omega-3 fatty acids and also contains antioxidant minerals for cardiovascular health. It is the ideal good mood food.

The firm and meaty flesh of tuna is popular even with nonfish lovers and is easy to cook. It is a healthy treat, too, because it is a good source of the omega-3 fatty acids EPA and DHA, which many research trials have shown are important for reducing the risk of blood clots as we age, and can, therefore, protect cardiovascular health. They can also improve brain function and alleviate depression. Tuna contains three other mood enhancing nutrients. The first of these is the amino acid tryptophan, which converts to the calming chemical serotonin in our brains. The second is selenium, the antioxidant mineral thought to help lift depression, and the third is the B vitamins, vital for healthy nerves.

- Omega-3 fatty acids, which offer protection against cardiovascular disease and brain degeneration.
- High in tryptophan, which has a mood-enhancing effect.
- Selenium and the B vitamins reduce anxiety and lift depression.

Practical tips:
You can freeze fresh tuna, well wrapped, for 3–4 weeks. To retain all the health benefits of the omega-3 fatty acids, don't overcook it; for example, poach for 3 minutes, then flake into a salad or rice. Slice and stir-fry for a minute with vegetables and noodles, or cook for a minute or so on each side to retain a pink center.

DID YOU KNOW?

You should always try to eat fresh tuna. When the fish is canned, even in oil, it loses much of its omega-3 fatty acids.

MAJOR NUTRIENTS PER 3½ oz. TUNA

Calories	144
Protein	23 g
Total fat	4.9 g
EPA	0.4 g
DHA	1.2 g
Niacin	8.3 mg
Vitamin B6	0.5 mg
Vitamin B12	9.4 mcg
Vitamin E	1 mg
Potassium	252 mg
Selenium	36 mcg
Magnesium	50 mg
Iron	1 mg
Zinc	0.82 mg

Seared tuna with beans and artichokes

SERVES 6   (W)(B)(H)(M)(S)

⅔ cup extra virgin olive oil

juice of 1 lemon

½ tsp crushed red pepper

4 thin fresh tuna steaks, about
    4 ounces each

1¼ cups dried cannellini beans,
    soaked overnight

1 shallot, finely chopped

1 garlic clove, crushed

2 teaspoons finely chopped
    rosemary

2 tablespoons chopped
    flat-leaf parsley

4 oil-cured artichokes, quartered

4 vine-ripened tomatoes, sliced
    lengthwise into segments

16 ripe black olives, pitted

salt and pepper

lemon wedges, to serve

Method

1 Put ¼ cup of the olive oil in a
   shallow dish with 3 tablespoons
   of the lemon juice, the crushed
   red pepper, and ¼ teaspoon
   pepper. Add the tuna steaks
   and let marinate at room
   temperature for 1 hour,
   turning occasionally.

2 Meanwhile, drain the beans
   and put in a saucepan with
   plenty of fresh water to cover.
   Bring to a boil, then boil
   rapidly for 15 minutes. Reduce
   the heat slightly and cook for
   another 30 minutes, or until
   tender but not disintegrating.
   Add salt in the last 5 minutes
   of cooking.

3 Drain the beans and transfer
   to a bowl. While still warm,
   toss with ⅓ cup of the olive
   oil, then stir in the shallot,
   garlic, rosemary, parsley, and
   remaining lemon juice. Season
   with salt and pepper. Let
   stand for at least 30 minutes
   to let the flavors develop.

4 Heat 1 tablespoon olive oil
   in a saucepan until hot. Add
   the tuna and the marinade,
   and sear for 1–2 minutes on
   each side over high heat.
   Remove from the pan and let
   cool a little.

5 Transfer the beans to a
   serving dish. Mix in the
   artichokes, tomatoes, and
   olives, adding more oil and
   seasoning, if necessary. Flake
   the tuna and arrange on top.
   Serve immediately with lemon
   wedges for squeezing over.

60 SARDINES

Sardines are an inexpensive fish to choose for health during menopause. The special fats they contain offer an excellent range of benefits.

Sardines are packed with the two omega-3 fatty acids EPA and DHA, which are found in no other foods apart from fish and seafood. These fatty acids can help prevent or control diseases, including diabetes, arthritis, cardiovascular disease, and Alzheimer's. This makes them particularly useful in midlife and later years, while their ability to aid concentration and memory and to lift depression is of real benefit during menopause for women who have these symptoms. Sardines are one of the few foods that are rich in vitamin D, which helps calcium to be absorbed by our bodies and keep bones healthy after menopause. They are also high in iron, essential for healthy blood, energy, and a smooth-running brain. Sardines are a good source of vitamin E, a powerful antioxidant that supports a healthy heart and skin. Sardines are rich in selenium, too, which lifts depression and may help prevent cancer.

- Excellent source of omega-3 fatty acids, which protect us from disease.
- EPA and DHA help memory, mood, and concentration.
- Bone and skin protective and anticancer.
- Rich in a range of minerals and antioxidants.

Practical tips:
If you dislike their small bones, buy sardines already filleted. The bones are edible, however, and a good source of calcium. Canned sardines retain much of the nutrient profile of fresh ones.

DID YOU KNOW?

Ounce for ounce, sardines provide more protein than steak, more potassium than bananas, and more iron than cooked spinach.

MAJOR NUTRIENTS PER 3 AVERAGE-SIZE SARDINES

Calories	280
Protein	33 g
Total fat	16 g
EPA	1.1 g
DHA	1.5 g
Niacin	7 mg
B12	15 mcg
Vitamin D	1,108 IU (27.7 mcg)
Vitamin E	2.7 mg
Potassium	536 mg
Selenium	71 mcg
Magnesium	53 mg
Iron	3.9 mg
Zinc	1.8 mg

Broiled sardines with Mediterranean spinach

SERVES 4–6   (W) (B) (H) (M) (S)

½ cup olive oil, plus extra for
    brushing and oiling
finely grated rind and juice of
    1 orange
1 small red onion, thinly sliced
1 garlic clove, finely chopped
1 small red chile, seeded and finely
    chopped, or pinch of crushed
    red pepper
12 sprigs fresh thyme
12 sardines, heads removed,
    gutted, and rinsed inside
    and out

Mediterranean spinach

1½ tablespoons olive oil
1 onion, chopped
1 large garlic clove
½ tablespoon ground coriander
½ tablespoon ground cumin
2 pounds baby leaf spinach
½ cup pine nuts, lightly toasted
salt and pepper

Method

1 Put the olive oil, orange rind and juice, onion, garlic, and chile in a flat bowl large enough to hold all the sardines and beat until blended. Put a thyme sprig inside each sardine, then add the fish to the marinade and use your hands to coat them.

2 To make the Mediterranean spinach, heat the oil in a skillet over medium–high heat. Add the onion to the skillet, and cook, stirring, for 3 minutes, then crush the garlic, add to the skillet, and continue to cook, stirring, until the onion is soft. Stir in the coriander and cumin with a pinch of salt and continue to cook, stirring, for 1 minute. Add the spinach with just the water clinging to its leaves, using a wooden spoon to push it into the skillet. Season with salt and pepper. Cook, stirring, for 8 minutes, or until the leaves are wilted. Sprinkle with the pine nuts, then cover and keep warm while you broil the sardines.

3 Preheat the broiler to high. Line the broiler pan with aluminum foil and lightly brush with oil. Arrange the sardines on the pan and place them 4 inches beneath the heat. Broil for 1½ minutes. Use a spatula to turn the fish over. Brush with oil, then broil for 1½–2 minutes, until the fish is cooked through and the flesh flakes easily.

4 Serve the sardines accompanied by the Mediterranean spinach.

61

CHEDDAR CHEESE

Many women shun cheese, believing it isn't a healthy food. However, hard cheese, such as cheddar, has many benefits during menopause and after.

It's true that whole hard cheese contains a high proportion of its fat as saturates, but if you choose the reduced-fat types, the fat content is manageable and the benefits the cheese offers are many. Cheddar cheese is rich in calcium, a small serving providing half of your day's needs. This mineral is the major constituent of bones and essential to maintaining bone density and strength during and after menopause. Cheese also contains phosphorous, which binds with calcium to form bones and teeth, and some vitamin D, vital for bone formation. Hard cheese is ideal for women trying to lose weight or avoid gaining, as several studies have found that calcium-rich foods speed up the metabolic rate, helping us to burn fat. The casein in cheese also helps boost metabolism, while the high-protein content keeps hunger away. A high-calcium diet can even lower the risk of breast cancer. Hard cheese is a good source of iodine, too, which helps the thyroid function, and one of the few good nonvegan sources of vitamin B12.

- Calcium content maintains bone strength and density.
- Helps speed up the metabolic rate and burn fat.
- Helps lower the risk of breast cancer.

Practical tips:
Shred cheddar over meals and soups or make a cheese sauce to top vegetables. Buy hard cheese in bulk to save money, cut into chunks, wrap, and freeze.

DID YOU KNOW?
Hard cheese contains fluoride and phosphorous, minerals that help to keep teeth and gums healthy. Eating cheese after a meal is better than eating an apple to maintain a healthy PH balance.

MAJOR NUTRIENTS PER ½ CUP SHREDDED (1¾ OZ.) CHEDDAR CHEESE (16% FAT)

Calories	136
Protein	16 g
Total fat	8 g
Vitamin B12	0.6 g
Vitamin B2	0.3 mg
Folic acid	28 mcg
Vitamin D	3 IU
Calcium	420 mg
Selenium	5.5 mcg
Magnesium	20 mg
Potassium	55 mg
Zinc	1.4 mg
Phosphorous	310 mg
Fluoride	17.4 mcg

Cheddar biscuits

MAKES 12   Ⓑ

*4 sun-dried tomatoes
(not packed in oil)*
*2¾ cups all-purpose flour, plus
extra for dusting*
1 tablespoon baking powder
½ teaspon baking soda
½ teaspoon salt
½ teaspoon chipotle powder
½ teaspoon dry mustard
1 teaspoon dried basil
*6 tablespoons unsalted butter,
chilled, plus extra for greasing*
1¼ cups shredded cheddar cheese
¾ cup buttermilk

Method

1 Preheat the oven to 400°F. Grease a baking sheet and set aside. Soak the sun-dried tomatoes in a small bowl with hot water to cover for 10 minutes. Drain, squeeze out any excess liquid, and chop finely. Set aside.

2 In a large bowl, sift together the flour, baking powder, baking soda, and salt. Stir in the chipotle powder, mustard, and basil. Cut in the butter using a pastry blender or rub it in with your fingertips until completely incorporated. Fold in the cheese and sun-dried tomatoes. Using a kitchen fork, stir in the buttermilk. The dough will be slightly sticky. Gather the dough into a ball with your hands and turn out onto a well-floured surface. With floured hands, pat the dough to ½ inch thick and cut into 12 squares, using a floured knife.

3 Place the squares on the baking sheet with a little space between them and bake in the preheated oven for about 15 minutes, or until well risen and lightly browned. Remove from the oven and serve immediately.

62

YOGURT

Plain yogurt with live cultures is one of the best types of dairy produce you can eat for good health, especially during midlife, the menopausal years, and older age.

Yogurt has been eaten through the ages as an aid to long life and for its health-giving properties, and modern science has since backed this up with real proof. Yogurt with live cultures, which contains billions of bacteria, such as acidophilus and bifidobacteria, is a superb digestive aid. The "friendly" bacteria line the digestive tract and help to relieve bloating and constipation, protect the digestive system from harm, and boost the immune system. Yogurt also has many of the benefits of cheese and milk. Like them, it is high in calcium, which has several positive health properties, including calming the nerves, aiding sleep, and maintaining bone health. Yogurt appears to have almost magical fat-burning properties—including yogurt in your diet three times a day can boost fat loss and abdominal fat loss considerably, but also helps retain muscle tissue, loss of which is a common problem among dieters. A daily container of yogurt with live cultures has also been shown to improve the blood cholesterol profile, lowering LDL and raising HDL in women testers.

• Boosts digestive health and relieves constipation and bloating.
• Burns body fat, particularly abdominal fat, and builds muscle.
• Improves blood cholesterol profile and aids sleep.

Practical tips:
Yogurt is one of the best foods for snacking or for breakfast. Add chopped nuts or fruit for even more nutritional value.

DID YOU KNOW?

Yogurt is one of the most widely consumed nongrain foods across the world, being popular in Europe, India, the Middle East, Asia, and North America.

MAJOR NUTRIENTS PER ½ CUP (3½ FL OZ.) YOGURT

Calories	63
Protein	5.2 g
Total fat	1.5 g
Carbohydrate	7 g
Vitamin B12	0.5 mg
Vitamin B2	0.2 mg
Choline	15 mg
Calcium	183 mg
Magnesium	17 mg
Potassium	234 mg
Zinc	0.9 mg
Phosphorous	144 mg
Iodine	34 mcg
Fluoride	12 mcg

Fruity yogurt cups

MAKES 12   (W) (B) (H)

2 cups yogurt with live cultures
1½ tablespoons finely grated
*   orange rind*
2 cups mixed berries, such as
*   blueberries, raspberries, and*
*   strawberries, plus extra to*
*   decorate*
fresh mint sprigs, to decorate
*   (optional)*

Method

1 Set the freezer to rapid freeze at least 2 hours before freezing this
   dish. Line a 12-cup muffin pan with 12 paper cupcake liners, or use
   small ramekin dishes placed on a baking sheet. Mix together the
   yogurt and orange rind in a large bowl.

2 Cut any large strawberries into pieces so that they are the same size
   as the blueberries and raspberries. Add the fruit to the yogurt, then
   spoon into the paper liners or ramekins. Freeze for 2 hours, or until
   just frozen.

3 Decorate with extra fruit and mint sprigs, if using, and serve.
   Remember to return the freezer to its original setting afterward.

MILK

As a drink, low-fat milk makes a good alternative to water, being high in calcium and other nutrients that are important for women during menopause.

Calcium has many roles in women's health. It is vital for the nerves, the blood, and blood pressure regulation, as well as in its more familiar role in bone-building and maintenance. Calcium may also speed up the metabolic rate, and one large study found that drinking milk regularly may help the body to use insulin more efficiently and, thus, may help to prevent or control type 2 diabetes. Calcium has also been called "nature's tranquillizer," helping us to get a good night's sleep. Dairy produce is often thought of as not good for the heart, but new research appears to suggest that the opposite is true. Milk's whey proteins contain peptides that may be helpful in regulating our blood pressure, and it is a good source of the B vitamins, potassium, and magnesium, all also important in heart protection. Milk is useful for adding to any meal because its protein content helps slow absorption of the food and prevent hunger.

- Calcium content speeds up the metabolic rate and improves insulin sensitivity.
- Aids restful sleep and is traditionally used to calm the nerves.
- Contains several nutrients and chemicals that help protect the heart.

Practical tips:
Buy milk as fresh as you can so that it keeps longer without turning rancid—always store under 41°F. Use in a breakfast smoothie with banana and cinnamon, and have a cup of hot milk at bedtime.

DID YOU KNOW?

It is thought that cow's milk has been used as a drink for humans for over 6,000 years, with some of the earliest evidence emerging from the areas in the southeast Mediterranean.

MAJOR NUTRIENTS PER ½ CUP (3½ FL OZ.) SKIM MILK

Calories	34
Protein	3.4 g
Total fat	Trace
Carbohydrate	5 g
Vitamin B12	0.5 mg
Vitamin B2	0.2 mg
Calcium	122 mg
Magnesium	11 mg
Potassium	156 mg
Zinc	0.4 mg
Phosphorous	101 mg
Iodine	29 mcg

Spiced banana milkshake

SERVES 2 (**W**)(**B**)(**M**)

1½ cups skim milk

2 bananas

⅔ cup yogurt with live cultures

½ teaspoon allspice, and a pinch
   of allspice, to decorate

6 ice cubes (optional)

Method

1 Place the milk, bananas, yogurt, and allspice in a food processor
   or blender and process gently until smooth.

2 Pour the mixture into two glasses and serve with ice, if using.
   Add a pinch of allspice to decorate.

4

Grains and Beans

Whole grains, such as barley, rice, and oats, and beans, such as lentils, chickpeas, and soybeans, are staple foods throughout the world, and they are some of the least expensive foods you can buy. Nevertheless, they contain an amazing array of nutrients and chemicals that are helpful during menopause, as well as several types of fiber.

(W) Ideal for weight control

(F) High in fiber

(B) Protects and strengthens bones

(H) Heart health

(M) Mood booster

(S) Improves skin condition

64 **BARLEY**

Barley is a staple food for many people around the world. High in fiber and a source of several nutrients, it is a useful inclusion in a menopausal diet.

Choose whole-grain (pot) barley instead of pearl barley, which is highly milled and retains few of the nutrients and little fiber. The high fiber content of barley helps to lower harmful LDL cholesterol. The insoluble-fiber content speeds the passage of food through the digestive system, where it produces a compound called propionic acid, which helps reduce the amount of cholesterol produced by the liver. Beta-glucans, a type of soluble fiber in the grain, also lowers cholesterol by binding to it and removing it from the body. Vitamin B3 (niacin), present in high amounts, contributes to the cholesterol-lowering action. Barley also seems to be excellent at controlling blood-sugar levels and, like other whole-grain cereals, is thought to lower the risk of breast cancer, probably because of the lignans, fibers, and selenium it contains.

- Reduces levels of harmful blood cholesterol in several ways.
- Helps control blood sugar levels, which stops us feeling hungry and reduces the risk of type 2 diabetes.
- May reduce risk of breast cancer.

Practical tips:
Pot (Scotch) barley, available at health food stores, takes longer to cook than the milled grain. Simmer in water in a covered saucepan for 45 minutes, until tender. Or add to soups or stews, adding extra stock because the grains soak it up. Use the cooked grains cold in a salad, or try cracked or flaked barley as a hot breakfast cereal.

DID YOU KNOW?

Before wheat was widely grown in Europe, bread was made from barley and rye instead. These breads are still many people's favorites today.

MAJOR NUTRIENTS PER ⅔ CUP (3½ OZ.) COOKED POT BARLEY

Calories	124
Protein	4.4 g
Total fat	0.8 g
Carbohydrate	25.7 g
Fiber	6 g
Niacin	1.6 mg
Magnesium	47 mg
Potassium	158 mg
Zinc	1 g
Iron	1.2 mg
Selenium	13 mcg

Chicken and barley stew

SERVES 4　(W) (F) (M)

2 tablespoons vegetable oil

8 small, skinless chicken thighs

2 cups chicken stock

½ cup pot (Scotch) barley, hulled barley, or pearl barley, rinsed and drained

6 small new potatoes, unpeeled and halved lengthwise

2 large carrots, sliced

1 leek, sliced

2 shallots, sliced

1 tablespoon tomato paste

1 bay leaf

1 zucchini, sliced

2 tablespoons chopped fresh flat-leaf parsley, plus extra sprigs to garnish

1 tablespoon all-purpose flour

2 tablespoons water

salt and pepper

Method

1　Heat the oil in a large casserole dish over medium heat. Add the chicken and cook for 3 minutes, then turn over and cook on the other side for another 2 minutes. Add the stock, barley, potatoes, carrots, leek, shallots, tomato paste, and bay leaf. Bring to a boil, reduce the heat, and simmer for 30 minutes.

2　Add the zucchini and parsley, cover the dish, and cook for another 20 minutes, or until the chicken is tender and the juices run clear when the tip of a knife is inserted into the thickest part of the meat. Remove the bay leaf and discard.

3　In a separate bowl, mix the flour with the water and stir into a smooth paste. Add it to the stew and cook, stirring, over low heat for another 5 minutes. Season with salt and pepper.

4　Remove from the heat, ladle into serving bowls, and garnish with sprigs of fresh parsley.

65

OATS

Including oats in your diet on a regular basis will help control the symptoms of menopause and reduce your risk of heart disease and osteoporosis.

Oats alleviate menopausal symptoms, such as depression, anxiety, low mood, and insomnia, because they stimulate the production of serotonin, the "feel good" chemical in the brain. They are also rich in several of the B vitamins, which help to promote nerve health and good mood. They contain lignans, which can reduce the severity of hot flashes and night sweats, as well as the risk of breast cancer, and their high zinc content can improve libido. Oats contain a range of antioxidants and plant chemicals, including avenanthramides, saponins, and vitamin E, which are able to keep the heart and arteries healthy. In addition, their high beta-glucan content helps to reduce LDL cholesterol. Due to their fiber, fat, and protein content, oats are relatively low on the glycemic index, which means they are a particularly suitable grain for dieters, people with insulin resistance, and diabetics.

- One of the best grains to choose to reduce day-to-day menopausal symptoms.
- May reduce risk of cardiovascular disease and breast cancer.
- Good choice for dieters and diabetics because they are low on the glycemic index.

Practical tips:
Use rolled oats/oat flakes to make muesli, oatmeal, cookies, and crumble topping. Oat flour can replace part of the flour in baking. Use whole oats in casseroles instead of, for example, pearl barley.

DID YOU KNOW?

Oat bran, the outer layer of the grain, is rich in fiber and can be bought at health food stores. Add it to recipes or sprinkle it on yogurt or cereal.

MAJOR NUTRIENTS PER ½ CUP (1¾ OZ.) DRY ROLLED OATS

Calories	195
Protein	8.5 g
Total fat	3.5 g
Carbohydrate	33 g
Fiber	5.3 g
Folic acid	28 mcg
Thiamin	0.4 mg
Niacin	0.5 mg
Vitamin E	0.75 mg
Magnesium	88 mg
Potassium	214 mg
Zinc	2 g
Calcium	27 mg
Iron	2.3 mg

Apple and oat muffins

MAKES 12   **B** **H** **M**

1 cup all-purpose flour

1 tablespoon baking powder

1 teaspoon ground allspice

½ cup firmly packed light
    brown sugar

2 cups rolled oats

1 large apple, such as Jonagold,
    Pippin, or Rome, unpeeled

2 eggs

½ cup skim milk

½ cup fresh apple juice

⅓ cup sunflower oil

Method

1 Preheat the oven to 400°F. Line a 12-cup muffin pan with baking
cups. Sift together the flour, baking powder, and allspice into a large
bowl. Stir in the sugar and 1½ cups of the oats.

2 Finely chop the apples, discarding the cores. Add to the flour
mixture and stir together.

3 Lightly beat the eggs in a bowl then beat in the milk, apple juice,
and oil. Make a well in the center of the dry ingredients and pour
in the beaten liquid ingredients. Stir gently until just combined; do
not overmix.

4 Spoon the batter into the prepared muffin pan. Sprinkle the
remaining oats over the tops of the muffins. Bake in the preheated
oven for about 20 minutes, until well risen, golden brown, and firm
to the touch.

5 Let the muffins cool in the pan for 5 minutes, then serve warm
or transfer to a wire rack and let cool completely.

66 BROWN RICE

Brown rice—a complex carbohydrate—is a versatile whole grain that provides a range of nutrients and compounds for health and well-being in midlife.

Brown rice has specific benefits for women during menopause. Its carbohydrate, vitamin B, and magnesium content helps to increase levels of the mood-calming and sleep-inducing chemical serotonin in the brain. The wheat germ has a high zinc content that can alleviate night sweats, hot flashes, and dry skin. Brown rice also contains saponins, the plant chemicals that help to lower blood cholesterol. It is a good source of selenium, too, essential for boosting the immune system and for counteracting depression. Its fiber content makes it a medium–low glycemic index food, ideal in small servings for weight control by encouraging satiety. It also helps to regulate blood sugar levels in diabetics.

- Magnesium, B vitamin, and carbohyrate content increases production of the brain chemical serotonin to alleviate insomnia and anxiety.
- Zinc reduces hot flashes and dry skin.
- Saponins help to reduce harmful cholesterol levels.
- Useful for dieters and diabetics.

Practical tips:

Try eating a calcium-rich food, such as cheese, nuts, seeds, or tofu, with brown rice, because the calcium will work with the magnesium contained in the rice to help keep bones strong. Leftover cooked rice can be kept for a day or two in the refrigerator if you cool it quickly and reheat it thoroughly until piping hot.

DID YOU KNOW?

Rice is one of the least allergenic foods we eat, meaning that few people have an allergic reaction to it, and it is much less likely to cause stomach bloating and indigestion than wheat.

MAJOR NUTRIENTS PER 1 CUP (7 OZ.) COOKED BROWN RICE

Calories	222
Protein	5 g
Total fat	1.8 g
Carbohydrate	46 g
Fiber	3.6 g
Niacin	3 mg
Thiamin (vitamin B1)	0.2 mg
Vitamin B6	0.3 mg
Selenium	19.6 mcg
Magnesium	86 mg
Iron	0.8 mg
Zinc	1.3 g
Calcium	20 mg

Spicy chickpea and brown rice salad

SERVES 4   (F) (B) (H) (M)

½ tablespoon olive oil

1 teaspoon cumin seeds,
   gently crushed

½ teaspoon coriander seeds,
   gently crushed

1 red onion, sliced

¾ teaspoon garam masala
   (available in Asian grocery
   stores, or make your own by
   mixing equal parts ground
   cumin, black pepper, cloves,
   and nutmeg)

1½ cups brown rice

⅓ cup raisins

3½ cups simmering vegetable
   stock

1 (15-ounce) can chickpeas,
   drained and rinsed

⅓ cup chopped fresh cilantro, plus
   extra sprigs to garnish

2 tablespoons slivered almonds

1⅓ cups drained and crumbled
   feta cheese, to serve

Method

1 Heat the olive oil in a saucepan and add the cumin and coriander
   seeds. Cook for a minute before adding the onion. Sauté the onion
   for 2–3 minutes, then stir in the garam masala. Stir in the rice and
   raisins, making sure they are coated with the spices.

2 Pour in the stock and bring to a boil. Reduce the heat, then cover
   and simmer for 25 minutes, until all the stock is absorbed and the
   rice is cooked.

3 Stir in the drained chickpeas, cilantro, and slivered almonds. Remove
   from the heat, transfer to serving bowls, and serve, warm, or cold,
   topped with crumbled feta cheese and garnished with fresh cilantro.

67

NAVY BEANS

Navy beans are extremely rich in protein, fiber, and calcium and have several nutritional benefits for women during midlife and beyond.

MAJOR NUTRIENTS PER ½ CUP (3½ OZ.) COOKED NAVY BEANS

Calories	140
Protein	8.2 g
Total fat	0.6 g
Carbohydrate	26 g
Fiber	10.5 g
Folic acid	140 mcg
Niacin	0.65 mg
Choline	44.7 mg
Magnesium	53 mg
Potassium	389 mg
Zinc	1 mg
Calcium	69 mg
Iron	2.3 mg

Navy beans are a high fiber food, in general, and are among the highest foods in soluble fiber, the type that can lower blood cholesterol and help to keep blood-sugar levels from rising too rapidly after a meal. For this reason, and because the beans are low in fat and high in protein, they make a good addition to a diet for women who want to prevent weight gain, as well as for people with diabetes. The insoluble fiber content also helps to prevent constipation and irritable bowel syndrome (IBS), which are common problems for women during midlife. Navy beans are one of the best vegetarian sources of protein and calcium for healthy bones. They are also rich in the antiaging, antioxidant minerals magnesium, iron, and zinc and are a good source of the B vitamins, which can help ease anxiety.

- Fiber-rich beans, so they able to help with weight control and to lower blood cholesterol.
- Insoluble fiber content helps prevent constipation and IBS.
- A good source of calcium, needed for a healthy heart and strong bones.
- Rich in antioxidant minerals.

Practical tips:

Navy beans make an excellent addition to casseroles, and provide protein. They are also good pureed with olive oil and a little lemon juice and black pepper—try with lamb.

Chicken casserole

SERVES 4 (**H**) (**M**) (**B**)

1½ tablespoons butter

1 tablespoon olive oil

8 skinless chicken thighs

2 strips unsmoked bacon, chopped

2 onions, chopped

3 garlic cloves

2 celery stalks, chopped

2 carrots, chopped

1 (15½-ounce) can navy beans, drained and rinsed

3 bay leaves

1½ teaspoons chopped thyme leaves, plus extra sprigs to garnish

½ cup cherry tomatoes

4 cups chicken stock

salt and pepper

whole-grain bread, to serve

Method

1 Preheat the oven to 300°F. Melt the butter with the olive oil in a large, flameproof casserole dish. Add the chicken thighs and cook for 1–2 minutes, turning occasionally. Add the bacon and cook for another 1–2 minutes, until the chicken starts to brown. Remove the meat with a slotted spoon and reserve.

2 Cook the onions, garlic, celery, and carrots in the dish for 2 minutes. Add the navy beans and stir well before adding the bay leaves, thyme, tomatoes, and 3½ cups of the chicken stock. Season well, then bring to a boil. Reduce the heat and simmer for 10 minutes before returning the chicken and bacon to the casserole dish.

3 Cover and transfer to the preheated oven. Cook for 40 minutes, or until the chicken is tender and the juices run clear when the tip of a knife is inserted into the thickest part of the meat. (If the casserole is becoming too dry after 20 minutes, add more stock.)

4 Remove from the heat, then remove and discard the bay leaves. Ladle into serving bowls, and garnish with sprigs of fresh thyme. Serve with whole-grain bread.

68 CHICKPEAS

Chickpeas are a nutritious, low-cost source of protein. High in health-protecting fiber and plant compounds, they are a useful food for people wanting to lose weight.

Small, regular helpings of chickpeas may help with weight loss—participants in a large study found that they ate less, felt less hungry, and snacked less when chickpeas were included in their diet. One reason may be that chickpeas are an excellent source of dietary fiber, which slows down the absorption rate of foods. Fiber has other benefits—the insoluble type helps to prevent constipation and digestive disorders, such as bloating and irritable bowel syndrome (IBS), while soluble fiber controls and lowers blood cholesterol and helps prevent strokes and heart disease. Chickpeas are high in iron, an important antioxidant that maintains brain and blood health, and energy levels. They also contain isoflavones that protect against heart disease and cancer, saponins that lower cholesterol, and sterols that protect against breast cancer.

- Research has shown that chickpeas can help with weight loss.
- High in insoluble fiber and soluble fiber, which help protect against a range of diseases.
- Iron maintains energy levels and brain function as we age.
- Plant chemicals that reduce the risk of heart disease and cancer.

Practical tips:
Chickpeas can replace some or all of the meat in soups, stews, and casseroles. Raw chickpeas need to be soaked for several hours before cooking but canned chickpeas are just as good nutritionally. Hummus is a popular snack made from chickpeas.

DID YOU KNOW?
Chickpeas can be cooked and ground into a type of flour, called chickpea, besan, or gram flour. This flour is used widely in Middle Eastern and Indian cooking and is a high-protein alternative to wheat.

MAJOR NUTRIENTS PER ⅔ CUP (3½ OZ.) COOKED CHICKPEAS

Calories	164
Protein	8.9 g
Total fat	2 g
Carbohydrate	27 g
Fiber	7.6 g
Folic acid	172 mcg
Magnesium	48 mg
Potassium	291 mg
Zinc	1.5 g
Calcium	49 mg
Iron	2.9 mg

Chickpea and cilantro fritters

SERVES 4   Ⓦ Ⓕ Ⓗ

1 cup all-purpose flour
1½ teaspoons baking powder
1 egg
¾ cup low-fat milk
5 oz scallions, thinly sliced
1 (15-ounce) can chickpeas,
    drained and rinsed
¼ cup chopped cilantro
sunflower oil, for frying
salt and pepper
fresh cilantro sprigs, to garnish

Method

1 Sift the flour and baking powder into a bowl and make a well in the center. Add the egg and milk and stir into the flour, then beat to make a smooth batter.

2 Stir in the scallions, chickpeas, and cilantro, then season well with salt and pepper.

3 Heat the oil in a large, heavy skillet and add tablespoonfuls of the batter. Cook in batches for 4–5 minutes, turning once, until the fritters are golden brown.

4 Serve the fritters stacked on serving plates, garnished with cilantro sprigs.

69 KIDNEY BEANS

Kidney beans are an excellent choice of food during menopause, containing good-quality protein, zinc, fiber, and a range of vitamins and minerals.

Kidney beans have a similar nutritional profile to soybeans but are lower in fat and higher in carbohydrate. They are invaluable for vegetarians because they are high in protein and minerals. They are also rich in both soluble and insoluble fiber: these help protect from cancers; give support to diabetics and people with insulin resistance by regulating blood sugar levels; and prevent hunger and also the accumulation of abdominal fat—a problem for many women after menopause. They contain good amounts of iron, which is necessary to prevent anemia and maintain energy levels, while the zinc content boosts the immune system and supports good skin and libido. Kidney beans are also high in potassium, which reduces bloating and high blood pressure.

- High fiber content helps regulate the release of insulin and to prevent hunger and abdominal fat.
- Provides protection against cancers.
- Extremely high in potassium, which minimizes fluid retention and controls high blood pressure.

Practical tips:
Red kidney beans are a traditional addition to chili con carne. To save time, use canned red kidney beans instead of the dried type, but rinse thoroughly under running water before cooking. Cooked kidney beans absorb other flavors well—try them marinated for 30 minutes in olive oil, lemon juice, and paprika.

DID YOU KNOW?

Raw (dried) kidney beans contain a potentially toxic substance (a form of lectin) that needs to be rendered harmless by boiling for at least 10 minutes, then drained and rinsed, before cooking.

MAJOR NUTRIENTS PER ½ CUP (3½ OZ.) COOKED KIDNEY BEANS

Calories	127
Protein	8.7 g
Total fat	0.5 g
Carbohydrate	23 g
Fiber	6.4 g
Folic acid	130 mcg
Niacin	0.6 g
Magnesium	42 mg
Potassium	405 mg
Zinc	1 mg
Calcium	35 mg
Iron	2.2 mg

Kidney bean risotto

SERVES 4　(W)(H)(M)

¼ cup olive oil

1 onion, chopped

2 garlic cloves, finely chopped

1 cup brown rice

2⅔ cups simmering vegetable
　stock

1 red bell pepper, seeded and
　chopped

2 celery stalks, sliced

3 cups thinly sliced cremini
　mushrooms

1 (15-ounce) can red kidney beans,
　drained and rinsed

3 tablespoons chopped fresh
　parsley, plus extra to garnish

½ cup cashew nuts

salt and pepper

Method

1　Heat half the oil in a large, heavy saucepan. Add the onion and cook, stirring occasionally, for 5 minutes, or until softened. Add half the garlic and cook, stirring frequently, for 2 minutes, then add the rice and stir for 1 minute, or until the grains are thoroughly coated with the oil.

2　Add the stock along with a pinch of salt and bring to a boil, stirring continuously. Reduce the heat, cover, and simmer for 35–40 minutes, or until all the liquid has been absorbed.

3　Meanwhile, heat the remaining oil in a heavy skillet. Add the bell pepper and celery and cook, stirring frequently, for 5 minutes. Add the sliced mushrooms and the remaining garlic and cook, stirring frequently, for 4–5 minutes.

4　Stir the rice into the skillet. Add the beans, parsley, and cashew nuts. Season with salt and pepper and cook, stirring continuously, until hot. Transfer to a serving dish, sprinkle extra parsley over the top, and serve immediately.

70

LENTILS

Lentils are a nutritious and versatile ingredient. The green, brown, or black types are the best to eat because they are richer in nutrients than red lentils.

Lentils are a useful food during menopause and in the postmenopausal years because they contain lignan, a plant compound that has been shown to act in a similar way to estrogen in our bodies, helping to reduce symptoms, such as hot flashes and night sweats. Lignan can also lower the risk of hormone-related cancers and protect against osteoporosis. Green and brown lentils are a particularly rich source of dietary fiber, both insoluble and soluble, which helps protect us against cancer and cardiovascular disease. They also contain plant chemicals called isoflavones, which offer similar protection. Lentils in general are rich in the B vitamins, which can help to improve mood, and a good source of all the major minerals, with a particularly high level of iron, and of zinc, which is a hormone regulator and immune booster.

- High in lignan, which can help minimize menopausal symptoms.
- Rich in dietary fiber, providing protection from cardiovascular disease and cancers.
- Contain a range of the B vitamins, improving mood and well-being.

Practical tips:
Because they don't need soaking before cooking, dried lentils are the beans to choose if you are short of time. Simmer in water for about 30 minutes, until soft. You can use them to make a soup with vegetables, or as a substitute for meat in dishes such as chili, casseroles, and lasagna.

DID YOU KNOW?

A number of foods, including lentils, contain purines. These are substances that can induce bouts of gout in susceptible people.

MAJOR NUTRIENTS PER ½ CUP (3½ OZ.) COOKED GREEN OR BROWN LENTILS

Calories	105
Protein	8.8 g
Total fat	0.7 g
Carbohydrate	17 g
Fiber	3.8 g
Folic acid	30 mcg
Niacin	0.6 mg
Vitamin B6	0.3 mg
Magnesium	34 mg
Potassium	310 mg
Zinc	1.4 mg
Calcium	22 mg
Iron	3.5 mg
Selenium	40 mcg

Lentil and vegetable casserole

SERVES 4 (W) (H) (M)

10 cloves
1 onion
1¼ cups green lentils
1 bay leaf
6½ cups vegetable stock
2 leeks, sliced
2 potatoes, diced
2 carrots, chopped
3 zucchini, sliced
1 celery stalk, chopped
1 red bell pepper, seeded
    and chopped
1 tablespoon lemon juice
salt and pepper

Method

1 Preheat the oven to 350°F. Press the cloves into the onion. Put the lentils into a large casserole dish, add the onion and bay leaf, and pour in the stock. Cover and cook in the preheated oven for 1 hour.

2 Remove the onion and discard the cloves. Slice the onion and return it to the casserole dish with the vegetables. Stir thoroughly and season with salt and pepper. Cover the dish and return to the oven for 1 hour.

3 Remove and discard the bay leaf. Stir in the lemon juice and serve straight from the casserole dish.

71 SOYBEANS

Soybeans are one of the best beans to eat throughout menopause because they are rich in minerals and plant chemicals that can alleviate symptoms and health issues.

Soybeans are one of the few plant sources of complete protein, containing all nine essential amino acids that comprise the protein in our diet. This protein is a good source of tryptophan, the amino acid that can convert to the mood-enhancing chemical serotonin in the brain. Soybeans are rich in plant chemicals that, when consumed regularly, can reduce menopausal symptoms, such as hot flashes and night sweats. These compounds also offer protection from breast and other hormonal cancers and heart disease. Soybeans are high in fiber, which supports a healthy digestive system and lowers blood cholesterol. They also contain iron, needed to prevent anemia and tiredness, and which can improve memory. Soybeans are also an important plant source for potassium, which reduces fluid retention and high blood pressure.

- Able to calm our mood due to their tryptophan content.
- Rich in plant compounds that can reduce menopausal symptoms and protect against hormone-based cancers.
- May improve memory function and counteract fluid retention.

Practical tips:
Use beans in soups and casseroles, mash for a dip, or add to vegetable burgers. Replace some of the wheat flour in baking with soy flour to increase protein, fiber, and nutrient content. Tofu is made from processed soybeans and is a good low-fat and low-sodium alternative to the whole beans, ideal for stir-fries.

DID YOU KNOW?

Soybeans can be eaten fresh. They are often sold frozen in pods in supermarkets, labeled as edamame. When fresh and shelled, they are pale green and can be used in the same way as fava beans or peas. The pods can also be cooked.

MAJOR NUTRIENTS PER ½ CUP (3½ OZ.) COOKED SOYBEANS

Calories	141
Protein	14 g
Total fat	7.3 g
Carbohydrate	5 g
Fiber	6 g
Folic acid	111 mcg
Thiamin	0.26 mg
Riboflavin	0.15 mg
Niacin	1.25 mg
Calcium	83 mg
Magnesium	63 mg
Potassium	510 mg
Zinc	0.9 g
Iron	3 mg

Soybean and mushroom salad

SERVES 2   (W) (H) (M)

1¼ cups shelled edamame
¾ cup sliced closed-cup
   mushrooms
2 cups baby spinach
handful of arugula

Dressing

3 tablespoons light olive oil
1½ tablespoons lemon juice
½ teaspoon Dijon mustard
1 tablespoon snipped fresh chives
1 tablespoon chopped fresh
   flat-leaf parsley
salt and pepper

Method

1 Steam the edamame in a steamer or metal colander set over a
saucepan of simmering water for 5–6 minutes, until just tender.
Rinse with cold water, drain well, and transfer to a serving bowl.
Add the mushrooms, spinach, and arugula and gently toss together.

2 To make the dressing, place all the ingredients in a bowl and beat
together. Pour the dressing over the salad and toss well to mix.
Serve immediately with extra pepper.

5

Herbs, Spices, and Health Foods

Almost all herbs and spices—from curry powder to
chiles, from parsley to rosemary—are extremely rich in
antioxidants, which help alleviate a range of menopausal
problems and symptoms. In this chapter, we also look at the
power of other health foods, such as green tea, maca, and
manuka honey, which have a range of beneficial effects
during menopause.

(W) Ideal for weight control

(F) High in fiber

(B) Protects and strengthens bones

(H) Heart health

(M) Mood booster

(S) Improves skin condition

72

CURRY POWDER

Adding a spoonful or two of a store-bought or homemade curry spice blend to your meal may be one of the best things you can do for your health in midlife.

A typical curry powder blend will contain, in varying amounts, most of the following spices: turmeric, cumin, coriander seed, cayenne pepper, ginger, and mustard seed. It may also include cloves, cardamom, nutmeg, mace, and other spices, usually in small amounts. The major ingredients are all powerful antioxidants that will help reduce the signs of aging, and are nutrient rich. A typical curry spice blend contains significant amounts of most of the important minerals for midlife health. There's potassium to help prevent fluid retention and control blood pressure; calcium and magnesium for healthy bones and heart and to promote restful sleep; iron for brainpower and energy; and zinc to regulate hormones and improve skin condition. The individual components also contain their own beneficial plant chemicals.

- Rich in a range of health-giving minerals and plant chemicals.
- Calcium and magnesium strengthen bones and protect the heart.
- Provides iron for brain function and energy, and zinc for hormonal and skin health.
- Anti-inflammatory and anticarcinogenic.

Practical tips:
If you have an electric grinder, make your own curry powder as required, from whole seeds (these store better and retain more nutrients than store-bought powder). Discard curry powder after six months; it may turn rancid because of the volatile oils it contains.

DID YOU KNOW?

Spices may be the plant's seed, bark, flower, fruit, or root. Many centuries ago, spices were prized worldwide and were one of the earliest foods to be traded on a global level.

MAJOR NUTRIENTS PER ¼ CUP (1 OZ.) CURRY POWDER

Calories	58
Protein	2.4 g
Total fat	2.7 g
Carbohydrate	6.5 g
Fiber	5.7 g
Niacin	0.9 mg
Potassium	457 mg
Calcium	160 mg
Iron	14.5 mg
Magnesium	70 mg
Zinc	1 mg

Vegetable curry

SERVES 6 (W) (F) (H) (M)

2 lemongrass stalks

¼ cup vegetable oil

3 large garlic cloves, crushed

1 large shallot, thinly sliced

2 tablespoons Indian curry powder

3 cups coconut milk

2 cups coconut water (not coconut
   milk) or vegetable stock

1 tablespoon Thai fish sauce

4 fresh red Thai chiles

6 kaffir lime leaves

1 carrot, cut diagonally into ½-inch
   thick pieces

1 small–medium eggplant,
   cut into 1-inch pieces

1 small–medium bamboo shoot,
   cut into thin wedges

2 cups snow peas

12 large shiitake mushrooms,
   stems discarded, caps halved

3 cups drained, and cubed tofu
   (1-inch pieces)

12 fresh Thai basil leaves, lightly
   crushed, or 3 tablespoons
   fresh cilantro leaves, and fried
   shallots, to garnish

Method

1 Discard the bruised leaves and root ends of the lemongrass stalks, then slice 6–8 inches of the lower stalks paper thin.

2 Heat the oil in a large saucepan over high heat, add the garlic and shallot, and stir-fry for 5 minutes, or until golden. Add the lemongrass and curry powder and stir-fry for 2 minutes, or until fragrant. Add the coconut milk, coconut water, fish sauce, chiles, and lime leaves and bring to a boil. Reduce the heat to low, then add the carrot and eggplant, cover, and cook for 10 minutes.

3 Add the bamboo shoot, snow peas, mushrooms, and tofu and cook for another 5 minutes.

4 Serve, garnished with the basil leaves and fried shallots.

73 LEMON BALM

Lemon balm has soft lemon-scented leaves. The leaves make a pleasant tea and contain a volatile oil known for its ability to calm the nerves, cool the body, and aid digestion.

As long ago as the fifteenth century, lemon balm leaves were steeped in boiling water to make a tea that was called "the elixir of life" and "the sovereign for the brain, powerfully chasing away melancholy" by the writers of the day. Over the centuries, the herb has been used to treat various symptoms, but its main use is to alleviate anxiety, nervousness, and depression, because the oils appear to have relaxing and calming properties. It may also aid restful sleep. Lemon balm is thought to ease tension headaches and palpitations, and may help to minimize the severity of hot flashes. It is used as a digestive aid, acting as a relaxant for the whole digestive system. With an ORAC score of 5,997 in its fresh form, lemon balm also contains a useful range of antioxidant compounds.

- Long known for its calming and mood-enhancing effect.
- May help reduce the incidence and severity of hot flashes.
- Acts as a digestive aid.

Practical tips:
To make a tea, add 2 tablespoons of fresh leaves to 1¼ cups of boiling water, steep for 5 minutes, strain, and drink hot or cold. Add slices of lemon, if desired. Use small leaves in fruit salads or as a garnish for drinks. Chop and stir into plain yogurt for use with a curry dish instead of raita. The plants are easy to grow, and the leaves can be dried, although they will lose some of their potency. They can also be frozen, but only for use as a tea.

DID YOU KNOW?

Lemon balm is widely used in Spain, where the leaves are a common ingredient in many game and fish dishes, and in herb vinegars.

MAJOR NUTRIENTS

There are no nutrients listed in the standard reference, the USDA Database, at this time.

Lemon balm loaf

MAKES 1 LOAF (M)(F)

butter, for greasing
2¼ cups whole-wheat flour
½ teaspoon baking powder
¾ cup sugar
grated rind of ½ lemon
2 tablespoons chopped lemon
  balm leaves
⅔ cup plain yogurt
⅔ cup peanut oil
3 eggs, beaten
⅔ cup blueberries

Method

1 Preheat the oven to 375°F. Grease and line an 8½-inch loaf pan with parchment paper.
2 Place the dry ingredients into a large bowl with the lemon rind and chopped lemon balm.
3 Beat together the plain yogurt, oil, and eggs, then stir the wet ingredients into the dry ingredients.
4 Lightly crush the blueberries to burst them, then stir them into the cake batter.
5 Pour the batter into the prepared pan and bake for 1 hour, until the tines of a fork inserted into the center comes out clean. Remove from the pan and let cool on a wire rack before serving.

74

CHILES

Native to Central and South America, chiles pack a nutritional as well as a hot punch and the compound that causes the heat has specific benefits during midlife.

MAJOR NUTRIENTS
PER 3 TBSP. CHOPPED (1 OZ.)
FRESH RED CHILE

Calories	12
Protein	0.5 g
Total fat	Trace
Carbohydrate	2.6 g
Fiber	0.4 g
Vitamin C	43 mg
Niacin	0.4 mg
Potassium	97 mg
Iron	0.3 mg
Beta-carotene	160 mcg
Lutein/Zeaxanthin	213 mcg

All chiles contain capsaicin, the plant chemical that gives them their heat. Capsaicin is scientifically proven to reduce inflammation in the body and, because of this, can relieve the pain and inflammation associated with arthritis and may even delay its onset. Capsaicin also appears to block the production of some types of cancerous cells, can protect us against blood clots, and may be an effective treatment for cluster headaches. Red and yellow chiles are high in beta-carotene, which can also reduce the symptoms of osteo- and rheumatoid arthritis, while the high vitamin C content increases the spice's total antioxidant activity. Recent research shows that chile consumption helps to reduce the amount of insulin required to lower blood sugar after a meal, making it of use to diabetics and people with insulin resistance. Chile consumption also speeds up the metabolic rate, so regular consumption can help to control weight problems.

• Capsaicin relieves pain and inflammation associated with arthritis.
• Contains vitamin C and carotenes, both powerful antioxidants.
• Speeds up the metabolic rate, helping to control weight problems.

Practical tips:
Chiles dry well and retain good amounts of their antioxidants—just lie them out on racks or thick paper in a warm, dry room. Chopped chiles freeze well. For a milder chile taste, remove the seeds inside the chiles and discard before using.

Tuna with a chile crust

SERVES 4 (w) (h) (m)

1 small bunch fresh cilantro
or flat-leaf parsley
3–4 dried red chiles, crushed
2 tablespoons sesame seeds
1 egg white
4 tuna steaks, about
5–6 ounces each
2–3 tablespoons sunflower oil
salt and pepper
lime wedges, to serve

Method

1 Chop the cilantro, leaving a few leaves whole to garnish. Mix together the crushed chiles, chopped cilantro, and sesame seeds in a shallow dish and season with salt and pepper. Lightly beat the egg white with a fork in a separate shallow dish.

2 Dip the tuna steaks first in the egg white, then in the chile-and-herb mixture to coat. Gently pat the crust evenly over the fish with the palm of your hand, making sure that both sides of the steaks are well covered.

3 Heat the oil in a large, heavy skillet. Add the tuna and cook over medium heat for 4 minutes, then turn over carefully, using a spatula. Cook for another 4 minutes, then transfer to warm serving plates. Serve immediately with lime wedges and the reserved cilantro leaves.

75 ROSEMARY

The antioxidant compounds present in fresh rosemary are thought to help prevent the common diseases of midlife, including breast cancer.

Native to the Mediterranean, rosemary will grow as a perennial in the warmer regions of this country. Its needlelike leaves are filled with aromatic oils, and recent research at the U.S. Department of Agriculture has found that it is one of the top herbs for antioxidant activity, with an extremely high ORAC rating of 165,280. This means it is one of the best plant foods you can choose to reduce the risk of disease and to ward off the long-term effects of aging. Rosemary extract has been found to help boost skin condition and to block estrogens in the body, and so may help prevent estrogen-dependent breast cancers. It has also been shown to increase blood flow to the head and brain, and in traditional herbal medicine is used as a mental stimulant, for concentration, and a memory booster, as a general tonic, and to help lift depression. An infusion of rosemary (rosemary tea) is recommended by herbalists to treat rheumatism and digestive disorders.

- Strong antioxidant activity may help ward off midlife diseases.
- Believed to improve memory and mood.
- Traditional tonic for general ailments, and also helps digestion.

Practical tips:
Rosemary dries well and retains its antioxidant effects. Hang sprigs up to dry in a warm kitchen, then remove the leaves and store in an airtight container. Chop fresh rosemary leaves and use with other herbs, such as thyme, sage, and oregano, in casseroles.

DID YOU KNOW?

Rosemary is an evergreen shrub related to mint. In cooler climates, you can grow it indoors, but let the soil dry out a little before watering.

MAJOR NUTRIENTS
PER 2½ TBSP. (½ OZ.) CHOPPED
FRESH ROSEMARY

Calories	20
Protein	0.5 g
Total fat	0.9 g
Carbohydrate	3.1 g
Fiber	2 g
Folic acid	16 mcg
Magnesium	14 mg
Potassium	100 mg
Calcium	48 mg
Iron	1 mg

Mushroom and rosemary stroganoff

SERVES 4 (**W**) (**H**) (**S**) (**M**) (**B**)

2 tablespoons olive oil

1 large onion, diced

2 garlic cloves, finely chopped

1 leek, diced

1 pound wild mushrooms,
    coarsely chopped

3 large portobello mushrooms,
    sliced

1 teaspoon paprika

1 tablespoon chopped
    fresh rosemary

juice of ½ lemon

½ cup simmering vegetable stock

2 tablespoons crème fraîche
    or sour cream

salt and pepper

cooked brown rice, to serve

Method

1 Heat the oil in a large saucepan and sauté the onion, garlic, and leek until softened.

2 Add the mushrooms and paprika and toss well.

3 Add the rosemary and lemon juice and cook for a few minutes.

4 Pour in the vegetable stock and simmer until the liquid has been reduced by half.

5 Stir in the crème fraîche, season with salt and pepper, and serve immediately with freshly cooked rice.

76 SAGE

Sage is full of beneficial compounds, including oils that calm the body, minimize hot flashes, and slow the aging process. It may also improve memory.

In folk medicine, sage has one of the longest histories of use of any medicinal herb, and in recent years, scientific research has backed up this old faith. It is one of the highest plants on the ORAC scale, with a rating of 32,004 when fresh and 119,929 for dried. As such, sage is a powerful weapon against the free radicals that contribute to the aging process, because it is able to neutralize them before they can damage the body cells. Traditionally, sage has been used to reduce the number and strength of hot flashes during menopause, and as an aid to relaxation. It contains a variety of volatile oils, flavonoids, and phenolic acids, meaning it is strongly anti-inflammatory and may help relieve the pain of arthritis and keep our arteries healthy. In recent trials, sage was also found to significantly improve short-term memory.

- Fights the aging process by being strongly antioxidant and anti-inflammatory.
- May reduce the severity and frequency of hot flashes in many women.
- Recent research has found that it improves memory function.

Practical tips:
Sage leaves dry well. Hang up small branches in a hot, dry place until the leaves are crisp, then store in an airtight container. Add sage to other chopped herbs to make an herb omelet or stuffing. Try sprinkling chopped fresh sage on pizzas and pasta.

DID YOU KNOW?

Sage is native to countries in the Mediterranean region and has been used as a herb there since the time of the ancient Greeks, who regarded it as sacred.

MAJOR NUTRIENTS PER ¼ CUP CHOPPED (½ OZ.) FRESH SAGE

Calories	22
Protein	0.7 g
Total fat	0.9 g
Carbohydrate	4.2 g
Fiber	2.8 g
Folic acid	19 mcg
Magnesium	30 mg
Potassium	75 mg
Calcium	116 mg
Iron	1.9
Beta-carotene	244 mcg

Sage risotto

SERVES 4   (H) (M) (S)

4 tablespoons butter

1 onion, diced

1½ cups brown rice

3 tablespoons white wine

*5½ cups simmering vegetable
stock*

1½ cups quinoa

10–12 chopped fresh sage leaves

¾ cup grated Parmesan cheese

Method

1 Melt 3 tablespoons of the butter in a saucepan and sauté the onion
for 5–6 minutes, until soft.

2 Stir in the brown rice and cook for 1–2 minutes, then pour in the
wine. Boil until the wine has reduced by half, then pour in the
stock and bring to a boil again. Reduce the heat and simmer for
15 minutes.

3 Stir in the quinoa and sage and cook for another 10–12 minutes,
until the liquid has been absorbed and the rice and quinoa are
both cooked.

4 Stir in the remaining butter and grated Parmesan cheese. Transfer
to serving plates and serve immediately.

77 PARSLEY

Parsley is a traditional herbal remedy and one of the most nutritious of herbs. It is strongly antioxidant and contains several volatile oils.

Parsley is often used as a decorative garnish and discarded instead of eaten, but its leaves are both tasty and a good source of several nutrients. They contain the carotenes lutein and zeaxanthin, which protect our eyesight, and the antioxidant vitamin C, which improves skin and brain health and encourages the herb's iron content to be absorbed in the body. Parsley is also a good source of vitamin K, which helps calcium to be absorbed and do its job strengthening our bones. The seeds contain most of the beneficial oils, including myristicin, coumarins, alpha-thujene, and limonene, all of which have anticancer action. Parsley also contains a range of flavonoids, including apiin, which is diuretic and linked with relief from fluid retention, and luteolin, which is anti-inflammatory. An infusion of the leaves can help relieve pain from arthritis and rheumatism.

- A good source of vitamin C and iron, potassium, and folic acid.
- Lutein and zeaxanthin help prevent macular degeneration.
- Antioxidant, anticancer, and anti-inflammatory.
- High vitamin K content helps preserve bone density.

Practical tips:
Parsley keeps well on the stem for several days in a plastic bag in the refrigerator, or you can chop and freeze for use in cooking. To make tabbouleh, combine chopped parsley with mint, lemon juice, cooked bulgur wheat, and oil.

DID YOU KNOW?

Flat-leaf (Italian) and curly-leaf parsley have a similar nutritional profile. Parsley rates extremely highly on the ORAC scale, with a score of 73,670 for the dried herb, and 1,301 for fresh.

MAJOR NUTRIENTS PER 15 (½ oz.) FRESH PARSLEY SPRIGS

Calories	5
Protein	0.5 g
Total fat	Trace
Carbohydrate	1 g
Fiber	0.5 g
Vitamin C	20 mg
Vitamin K	272 mcg
Folic acid	23 mcg
Magnesium	8 mg
Potassium	83 mg
Calcium	21 mg
Iron	0.9
Beta-carotene	758 mcg
Lutein/Zeaxanthin	834 mcg

Mushrooms with parsley and olive oil

SERVES 4   (W) (H) (S)

1 pound mushrooms
½ cup extra virgin olive oil
2 garlic cloves, finely chopped
large handful of flat-leaf parsley,
*   chopped*
salt and pepper
sourdough toast, to serve

Method

1   Separate the mushroom heads from the stems. Coarsely chop the stems and set aside. Place a skillet over high heat and add the oil. When hot, add the mushroom caps and sauté. Check the undersides—when they begin to brown, turn them over. Season with salt and pepper.

2   Add the garlic, chopped mushroom stems, and parsley and sauté for 5–10 minutes, until the flavors really start to release and the garlic's bite eases a little.

3   Serve the mushrooms on slices of sourdough toast, with a drizzle of the hot oil from the skillet over them.

78

DARK CHOCOLATE

Cocoa beans contain a range of antioxidants, nutrients, and plant chemicals that can provide real benefits to women during menopause.

MAJOR NUTRIENTS PER 3 TBSP. (½ OZ.) COCOA POWDER

Calories	34
Protein	3 g
Total fat	2 g
Carbohydrate	8 g
Fiber	5 g
Niacin	0.3 mg
Calcium	19 mg
Potassium	229 mg
Magnesium	75 mg
Iron	2 mg
Zinc	1.02 mg
Phosphorous	110 mg
Theobromine	309 mg

MAJOR NUTRIENTS PER 3½ oz DARK CHOCOLATE (70% COCOA SOLIDS)

Calories	598
Protein	7.8 g
Total fat	42.6 g
Carbohydrate	46 g
Fiber	11 g
Niacin	1 mg
Vitamin E	0.6 mg
Calcium	73 mg
Potassium	716 mg
Magnesium	228 mg
Iron	12 mg
Zinc	3.3 mg
Phosphorous	308 mg
Theobromine	802 mg

Cocoa beans are a rich source of antioxidant flavonoids called catechins, which protect us against heart disease and cancer and may increase our metabolic rate. The chocolate-making process also produces procyanidins, which have an anti-inflammatory action and may reduce the symptoms of arthritis. Dark chocolate contains beta-sitosterol, a compound that helps prevent cholesterol from being absorbed in the body. Like cocoa, it also contains theobromine, which is a diuretic and dilates the blood vessels, as well as phenylethylamine (PEA), a stimulant that sharpens the brain. Tests show that chocolate increases the production of endorphins in the brain, which make us feel happy. Cocoa beans are rich in minerals—magnesium and phosphorous to keep bones strong; iron to improve brain function; zinc to boost libido; and potassium to regulate blood pressure.

- Compounds that protect us from heart and arterial disease.
- PEA and iron content can improve brain function, while endorphins improve mood.
- Contains theobromine and potassium, both of which are diuretic.
- Mineral content improves bone strength and libido.

Practical tips:
Look for chocolate with at least 70 percent cocoa solids, but eat it sparingly because cocoa butter is high in fat. Cocoa powder is low in fat but still contains the cocoa's fiber and nutrients.

Chocolate mousse

SERVES 4 (F) (B) (H) (M)

1 cup pitted dates
¾ cup dried figs
1 avocado, pitted and peeled
¼ cup agave syrup
1¼ cups unsweetened cocoa
*   powder*
¾ cup low-fat milk

Method

1 Place the dates, figs, and avocado in a food processor or blender and process briefly.
2 Add the agave syrup and cocoa powder and process again to form a thick paste.
3 Gradually pour in the milk and process again, continuing until you achieve a mousselike consistency.
4 Spoon the mousse into four glasses and chill in the refrigerator for 20 minutes before serving.

79 GREEN TEA

Green tea makes an excellent alternative to ordinary tea. Several cups a day may have an antiaging effect, help protect against several diseases, and speed up weight loss.

Green tea contains high levels of at least six different catechins. These antioxidant compounds, which give the tea its slightly bitter flavor, protect us against heart disease and cancers, and encourage weight loss by helping us burn fat. The caffeine, theobromine, and theophylline in green tea are also thought to boost the metabolism. L-theanine, an amino acid compound found in the tea, has been studied for its calming effects on the nervous system and may help with anxiety. Green tea is proven to improve heart health, too. Research shows that three or more cups a day lowers total cholesterol and raises "good" HDL cholesterol, while clinical studies in test tubes suggest that polyphenols in the tea inhibit the growth of breast cancer cells. This wonder drink, traditionally used to control blood sugar, may even help prevent the development of type 2 diabetes, as well as reduce the breakdown of cartilage associated with arthritis.

- Plant compounds assist heart health and inhibit breast cancer.
- Boosts the metabolism and encourages fat loss.
- May help improve the symptoms of arthritis.

Practical tips:
Green tea is made from the same plant as black tea, but the leaves are not fermented, which is why green tea contains more beneficial compounds. It is best enjoyed with just-boiled but not boiling water—let steep for 4 minutes before straining.

DID YOU KNOW?
Studies show that those who drink the most tea live the longest. Regular green tea consumption in women appears to reduce the risk of dying from a stroke by over 60 percent and of heart disease by over 30 percent.

MAJOR NUTRIENTS PER AVERAGE CUP GREEN TEA

Calories	2
Protein	0 g
Total fat	0 g
Carbohydrate	Trace
Magnesium	7 mg
Potassium	88 mg

Spiced poached pears in green tea

SERVES 2   (**W**) (**B**) (**H**) (**S**)

2 slightly underripe pears,
*   halved and peeled*
1 teaspoon lemon juice
3½ cups water
4 slices fresh ginger
2 star anise
1 cinnamon stick
1 tablespoon honey
2 green tea bags

Method

1 Using a melon baller or teaspoon, scoop out the core of each pear. Squeeze the lemon juice over the pears to prevent them from discoloring.

2 Bring the water to a boil in a large sauté pan. Reduce the heat to a simmer and add the ginger, star anise, cinnamon, and honey. Stir until the honey melts, then add the pears.

3 Simmer the pears for 15–20 minutes, partly covered, until tender, then remove from the pan using a slotted spoon. Increase the heat slightly, add the green tea, and simmer for about 5 minutes, until the cooking liquid has reduced and become syrupy.

4 Remove the spices and tea bags from the cooking syrup. Serve 2 pear halves per person with the syrup spooned over the top.

80

MANUKA HONEY

Dark-colored with a distinctive flavor, manuka honey is made by bees that feed on the nectar of the manuka trees in New Zealand.

Manuka honey is not only one of the best natural antibiotic foods that you can buy, it is also high in probiotic bacteria, which protect us against digestive disorders and constipation. It contains good amounts of antioxidants, particularly polyphenols, which can help improve cardiovascular health by binding with free radicals so that they can't damage our body cells. Regular consumption of raw honey, in general, has been shown to reduce harmful cholesterol, increase "good" HDL cholesterol, and lower blood homocysteine levels, a risk factor for heart disease. Raw honey also contains small amounts of bee propolis, a waxy substance from the hive that is thought to have antiaging properties. Research has found that eating raw honey may improve exercise performance and the speed with which we recuperate from activity, an important benefit in midlife when stamina and muscle power may decrease.

- Antibacterial and helps keep the digestive system healthy.
- Can improve our blood fat profile and protect against cardiovascular disease.

DID YOU KNOW?

Honey has been used since ancient times both as a food and as a medicine. Apiculture, the practice of beekeeping, dates back to at least 700 BC.

MAJOR NUTRIENTS PER 1 TBSP. (½ FL. OZ.) MANUKA HONEY

Calories	76
Protein	Trace
Total fat	Trace
Carbohydrate	20.6 g
Fiber	Trace

Practical tips:

Honey is best eaten as it is, served cold on bread, with yogurt, fruit, or cereal, or stirred into drinks. It may also be used instead of sugar or syrup in most recipes. Children under a year old should not eat honey because it may contain botulinum spores and toxins that can cause infant botulism.

Honey and yogurt dressing

SERVES 4   (W) (B)

1 tablespoon honey
⅓ cup low-fat plain yogurt
salt and pepper

Method

1 Put the honey and yogurt in a glass bowl and beat with a fork until thoroughly combined. Season with salt and pepper.

81

WHEATGRASS JUICE

This bright green liquid is thought to provide protection against disease, minimize the signs of aging, regulate blood-sugar levels, and improve digestion.

Wheatgrass juice contains a wide range of vitamins, enzymes, and plant nutrients that have been linked to disease prevention and specific health benefits. The polyphenols and flavonoids it contains are thought to provide protection from heart disease, while the green chlorophyll is believed to boost blood health and retard the growth of cancer cells. Chlorophyll may also be anti-inflammatory and antibacterial, and is thought to mop up harmful bacteria in the digestive system. Touted for its antiaging properties, there is anecdotal evidence that wheatgrass helps prevent hair from turning gray and can improve skin condition. There is also some evidence that regularly drinking wheatgrass juice can help regulate blood-sugar levels, making it ideal for diabetics and dieters.

• Contains antioxidants that help protect us from heart disease.
• May improve our blood profile and retard cancer growth.
• A digestive tonic, which may also improve hair and skin condition and regulate blood sugars.

Practical tips:
Wheatgrass juice has a strong taste that many people don't enjoy. Try it mixed with other vegetable juices, such as tomato and celery. You can sprout your own wheat at home easily and then cut the fresh green stalks to juice in a juicer or blender.

DID YOU KNOW?

Wheatgrass was first used as a health drink in the 1930s, after an agricultural chemist called Charles Schnabel fed wheatgrass to his chickens. The results were so convincing that he began making powdered wheatgrass for his family and friends.

MAJOR NUTRIENTS PER ½ CUP (3½ FL OZ.) WHEATGRASS JUICE

Calories	27
Protein	3 g
Total fat	Trace
Carbohydrate	3.6 g
Vitamin C	16 mg
Vitamin B12	Up to 1 mcg
Vitamin E	3 mg
Calcium	25 mg
Iron	2.3 mg
Magnesium	28.5 mg
Potassium	147 mg

Wheatgrass juice cleanser

SERVES 2 Ⓦ Ⓗ Ⓢ

3–4 carrots

1 beet

4 celery stalks

1 cucumber

½ lemon

small handful of fresh parsley
  or mint

¼ cup wheatgrass juice

water, to taste

celery stalks, to serve

Method

1 Chop all the vegetables to a size that fits your juicer.

2 Juice all the vegetables, lemon, and parsley. Add the wheatgrass juice and water to taste. Serve immediately with celery stalks.

82

MACA

Maca is native to the mountains of Peru, and is commonly used there as a vegetable. It is a pear-shaped root, often gold or black in color, with several medicinal uses.

Maca has been used as a herbal tonic for many years in Peru, and a recent scientific trial has found that it may help ease anxiety and depression in postmenopausal women and may also improve libido and sexual function. The plant has traditionally been used as a general health tonic, in particular, to treat fatigue, lack of energy and stamina, high blood pressure, osteoarthritis, and stress. Its active components are not well studied in Western laboratories, but the plant appears to contain glucosinolates and isothiocyanates, plant compounds known to help prevent cancers. Maca is rich in essential minerals, especially selenium, calcium, magnesium, and iron, all of which have important functions in midlife and as we age. The darker colored roots are also a good source of iodine, which can help thyroid function—an underactive thyroid gland can lead to weight gain, tiredness, and a condition called hypothyroidism.

- Research suggests that maca can alleviate anxiety and depression in menopause.
- May help beat fatigue and lack of stamina; acts as a general tonic.
- High in a range of minerals and cancer-fighting plant chemicals.

Practical tips:
Maca is hard to find outside Peru as a vegetable, so is usually bought dried from health food stores as a supplement, either in pill or powder form, or as a gelatin. Add powdered maca to smoothies, yogurt, or soups.

DID YOU KNOW?
Maca is sometimes known as "Peruvian ginseng" for its apparent ability to improve libido and stamina and restore vitality.

MAJOR NUTRIENTS
There are no nutrients listed in the standard reference, the USDA Database, at this time.

Energy snack bars

MAKES 10   (F) (M)

1¼ cups pecans

1 cup walnuts

¾ cup dates

3 tablespoons coconut oil

½ cup dried shredded coconut

1½ tablespoons maca powder

grated peel of 1 orange and
    juice of ½ orange

½ teaspoon molasses or honey

3 tablespoons ground flaxseeds

Method

1 Lightly grease a 7-inch-square baking pan. Place the pecans
   and walnuts in a food processor or blender and process until they
   resemble fine bread crumbs. Pour into a bowl and set aside.

2 Place the dates, coconut oil, dried coconut, maca powder, orange
   peel and juice, molasses, and flaxseeds in the processor. Process
   until the mixture becomes a thick paste. Return the nuts to the food
   processor and process until the mixture comes together.

3 Press into the prepared baking pan. Place in the refrigerator to chill
   for 1 hour.

4 Cut into 10 bars to serve. The bars can be stored in an airtight
   container in the refrigerator for up to two weeks.

83 BEE POLLEN

Bee pollen has been used as a health cure for centuries. It is said to promote longevity and energy, and to protect against diseases, including cancer.

Bee pollen comes from flowers that bees visit to find food. The pollen sticks to the bees' bodies as they help themselves to nectar, and is later collected from the beehives. It is said to be the richest source of micronutrients of any natural food, and contains all the vitamins and minerals that humans need for health. Bee pollen is said to improve stamina, strength, and vitality and to lift tiredness and low mood in menopausal women, and reduce anxiety. It contains many plant chemicals that are strongly antioxidant, including a range of flavonoids: rutin, which strengthens the capillaries and may prevent thread veins; quercetin, which protects heart health; and myricetin, which lowers LDL cholesterol. It is also thought to help with weight loss, add a glow to aging skin, reduce cravings, boost the immune system, and protect against cancer, although much of the evidence is circumstantial.

- Said to improve several symptoms of menopause, including tiredness, low mood, and anxiety.
- Taken as a general tonic, and may improve stamina and vitality.
- Contains plant chemicals linked with protection from heart disease and cancer.

Practical tips:
You can buy fresh bee pollen from some beekeepers but, for the national market, it is frozen or made into granules or capsules and sold in health food stores. These vary in quality and strength.

DID YOU KNOW?
Bee pollen is widely used as a treatment for hay fever and allergies, but if you are specifically allergic to pollen, avoid it because it could cause an extreme reaction.

MAJOR NUTRIENTS
There are no nutrients listed in the standard reference, the USDA Database, at this time.

Oatmeal with banana and bee pollen

SERVES 4 (W) (B) (H) (M)

2¼ cups rolled oats

3 cups milk

3 cups water

¼ cup plain yogurt

3 bananas, sliced

¼ cup bee pollen grains

Method

1 Place the oats in a saucepan, pour in the milk and water, and bring to a boil, stirring occasionally.

2 Simmer for 8–10 minutes, stirring from time to time, until the oatmeal thickens. Let stand for 1 minute.

3 Divide the oatmeal among four serving bowls. Top each serving of oatmeal with a dollop of plain yogurt, slices of banana, and a sprinkling of bee pollen.

84 WHEAT GERM

Wheat germ is the smallest, central part of the wheat grain, and it is full of nutrients. In its milled form, it makes an ideal food supplement during menopause.

As the embryo of the wheat kernel, the germ contains all the grain needs for life. It is packed with vitamins, most especially vitamin E, a powerful antioxidant that is known to protect the heart, and is also linked with cancer prevention, a reduction in hot flashes, and an improvement in memory and dry skin. Vitamin E also helps to control blood-sugar levels, which is an important factor for dieters and diabetics. The germ contains a similarly large amount of zinc, a useful mineral during menopause, because it can regulate the hormones and minimize symptoms, as well as boost libido. Other useful nutrients in wheat germ include magnesium for heart health and healthy bones; potassium for high blood pressure and fluid retention; and iron for energy and brain function. More than 5 percent of the fat content is omega-3 fatty acids, which have a range of health benefits, and are linked with a reduced risk of cardiovascular disease and Alzheimer's.

- Very rich in vitamin E, which protects the heart and alleviates menopausal symptoms.
- Zinc regulates hormones and improves libido and skin condition.
- Omega-3 fatty acids protect the brain and heart.

Practical tips:
Sprinkle onto breakfast cereal, fruit, or yogurt, and try it in soup or smoothies. Store it in the refrigerator because it easily turns rancid in warm conditions, and consume within a few weeks of purchase.

DID YOU KNOW?

Wheat is an ancient grain. Thought to originate in southwestern Asia, it has been consumed as a food for more than 12,000 years. It is only in the past century that refined white flour, which has no germ, has been popular in Western populations.

MAJOR NUTRIENTS PER HEAPING 1 TBSP. (⅓ OZ.) WHEAT GERM

Calories	71
Protein	5.3 g
Total fat	1.8 g
Carbohydrate	9 g
Fiber	3 g
Vitamin E	4.4 g
Niacin	0.9 g
Vitamin B6	0.7 g
Magnesium	54 mg
Potassium	190 mg
Zinc	3.4 mg
Iron	1.7 mg
Phosphorous	210 mg

Wheat germ, banana, and pumpkin seed muffins

MAKES 12   (F) (B) (M)

1 cup plus 2 tablespoons
*   all-purpose flour*
1 tablespoon baking powder
½ cup sugar
1¼ cups wheat germ
½ cup pumpkin seeds
2 bananas
about ⅔ cup skim milk
2 eggs
⅓ cup sunflower oil

Method

1 Preheat the oven to 400°F. Line a 12-cup muffin pan with baking cups. Sift together the flour and baking powder into a large bowl. Stir in the sugar, wheat germ, and ¼ cup of the pumpkin seeds.

2 Mash the bananas in a large bowl. Make up the puree to 1 cup with milk.

3 Lightly beat the eggs in a large bowl, then beat in the banana-and-milk mixture and the oil. Make a well in the center of the dry ingredients and pour in the beaten liquid ingredients. Stir gently until just combined; do not overmix.

4 Spoon the batter into the prepared muffin pan. Sprinkle the remaining pumpkin seeds over the tops of the muffins. Bake in the preheated oven for about 20 minutes, until well risen, golden brown, and firm to the touch.

5 Let the muffins cool in the pan for 5 minutes, then serve warm or transfer to a wire rack and let cool completely.

6

Nuts, Seeds, and Oils

Nuts, seeds, and plant oils should hold a special and regular place in our diet. High in healthy fats and protein, nuts and seeds have various formidable powers; for example, to help maintain bone mass and good skin condition, to prevent diabetes and heart disease, and even to promote weight loss or weight control.

(W) Ideal for weight control

(F) High in fiber

(B) Protects and strengthens bones

(H) Heart health

(M) Mood booster

(S) Improves skin condition

85

ALMONDS

Sweet almonds are extremely high in vitamin E, which can ease many symptoms of menopause. A small serving contains half the recommended daily intake.

Almonds are rich in the antioxidant vitamin E, a vitamin shown to protect against hot flashes, night sweats, dry skin, cancer, and coronary heart disease. It can also help reduce the pain of osteoarthritis and may improve memory. Because of their high fat content, almonds take a long time for the body to digest, so they keep us feeling full. Several research trials agree that nuts help control appetite and are a useful tool for dieters. Almonds are higher than almost any other plant food, weight for weight, in calcium, making them a good addition to the diet of women who don't eat dairy produce and need protection from osteoporosis. Almonds are a good source of monounsaturated fats, which help to improve our blood cholesterol profile, reducing levels of harmful LDL and increasing beneficial HDL.

• Vitamin E, which can minimize several menopausal symptoms.
• Keep hunger and weight gain at bay and blood-sugar levels stable.
• Good source of nondairy calcium for strong bones, and of monounsaturated fat for improved blood cholesterol profile.

Practical tips:
Almonds need to be stored in cool, dry conditions—in the dark is ideal. Buy whole almonds still in their shells or, at least, unblanched, for maximum nutrients. Almonds are ideal partners for chicken, rice, and apricots. Why not try a salad including all three?

DID YOU KNOW?

Almonds are the pitlike seeds of the fruit of a tree related to peaches and plums. They probably originated in north Africa or western Asia, and were first written about over 2,000 years ago.

MAJOR NUTRIENTS PER 3 TBSP. (1 OZ.) SHELLED ALMONDS

Calories	177
Protein	6.4 g
Total fat	15.7 g
Carbohydrate	5.6 g
Fiber	3 g
Vitamin E	7.4 mg
Niacin	1 mg
Calcium	71 mg
Potassium	198 mg
Magnesium	80 mg
Iron	1 mg
Zinc	0.9 mg

Rice paper wraps with almonds and pistachios

SERVES 4   (**H**) (**B**)

⅓ cup blanched almonds

2 tablespoons pistachio nuts

3 tablespoons honey

2 cups one-day-old fresh
    bread crumbs

zest of ½ orange

1 tablespoon sesame oil

4 round sheets Asian rice paper

strips of orange peel, to decorate

Method

1   Heat the nuts in a dry, nonstick skillet over medium–high heat.
    Remove from the skillet as soon as they begin to color.

2   Heat the honey in a saucepan over low heat; add the nuts, bread
    crumbs, orange zest, and sesame oil. Stir continually for 5 minutes,
    until the mix thickens to a paste. Remove from the heat and let cool.

3   Place the rice papers on a flat surface and brush with warm water;
    they will soften and become pliable after a few minutes. Divide the
    nut mixture among the rice papers, placing in the middle in a
    cylinder shape. Fold over the ends, roll up carefully, and serve,
    decorated with orange peel.

86

CASHEW NUTS

Sweet, mild-tasting cashew nuts make a healthy snack during menopause because they contain several nutrients that are of particular benefit during this time.

Cashew nuts, being lower in calories and total fat than most other nuts, are a good choice for snacking during menopause, when weight gain is common. One reason that nuts are thought to help keep weight under control is that they have a positive effect on postmeal blood sugars, lessening sugar surges and the release of insulin. They are also high in the B vitamins, a group that helps to protect women from heart and arterial disease, both of which increase significantly from the menopausal years onward. One large trial found that nut butter consumption decreased deaths from these causes by up to one-fifth. Cashew nuts are particularly high in oleic acid, the type of fat found in olive oil, and this, too, offers protection from cardiovascular disease. Cashew nuts are also a good source of magnesium, zinc, and iron, a trio of nutrients that offer specific protection to women at this stage of life.

- Lower-calorie, lower-fat, high-protein nut; ideal for dieters.
- Control postmeal sugar surges and the release of insulin.
- Offer several means of protection from cardiovascular disease.

Practical tips:
You can use cashew nuts in place of peanuts to make nut butter at home. Or add a handful to a vegetable stir-fry at the end of cooking, or toss into salads. Raw cashew nuts are much more beneficial to health than roasted ones, because heat destroys some of the valuable nutrients.

DID YOU KNOW?
In Brazil, where the cashew nut originates, cashew trees were long prized for their wood, not their nuts. It was only when imports to Europe began that the nuts became popular as a food.

MAJOR NUTRIENTS
PER 3 TBSP. (1 OZ.) SHELLED
CASHEW NUTS

Calories	166
Protein	5.5 g
Total fat	13 g
Carbohydrate	9 g
Fiber	1 g
Thiamin (B1)	0.1 mg
Niacin	0.3 mg
Vitamin B6	0.12 mg
Potassium	198 mg
Magnesium	88 mg
Iron	2 mg
Zinc	1.7 mg

Gingered tofu and cashew nut stir-fry

SERVES 4   (**W**) (**F**) (**B**) (**H**) (**S**)

1 tablespoon coconut oil
1½-inch piece fresh ginger, diced
3 scallions, sliced
2 garlic cloves, chopped
1 red bell pepper and 1 yellow bell
    pepper, seeded and sliced
2 carrots, cut into sticks
1½ cups snow peas
1 cup cashew nuts
½ Chinese cabbage, shredded
¼ cup bean sprouts
1¼ cups tofu cubes
1 tablespoon light soy sauce
1 teaspoon sesame oil

Method

1 Heat the coconut oil in a large wok. Add the ginger, scallions, and garlic and stir-fry for 2–3 minutes.

2 Add the bell peppers, carrots, snow peas, and cashew nuts, and stir-fry for another 4–5 minutes.

3 Add the Chinese cabbage, bean sprouts, tofu, soy sauce, and sesame oil. Stir-fry for 4–5 minutes, then cover and let steam for another 3–4 minutes.

4 Uncover and stir-fry for 1 minute before serving immediately.

87

BRAZIL NUTS

Brazil nuts are an astonishingly rich source of the mineral selenium, which has been shown to fight the diseases of aging, and alleviate low moods.

Brazil nuts contain more fat than almost any other type of nut, but much of it is the beneficial monounsaturated kind, and much of the remainder is omega-6 linoleic acid, which is essential for general good health and disease prevention. Brazil nuts have an extremely high content of selenium, which has anticancer properties and can alleviate depression. Many women do not have sufficient intake of this mineral, but just one or two Brazil nuts will provide a whole day's recommended intake. They are a good source of magnesium, which supports heart health, and zinc, known as the hormone-regulating mineral and so helpful for hot flashes and night sweats. Brazil nuts are high in fiber, too, which means they keep you feeling full and prevent constipation, and they are a good source of bone-building calcium and the antioxidant vitamin E.

- Antioxidant, antiaging, and anticancer.
- Extremely rich in selenium, the mood boosting, anticancer mineral, which can be in short supply in our modern diets.
- High magnesium content protects heart and bones.
- A good source of vitamin E, which keeps skin young.

Practical tips:
Keep unshelled nuts in a cool, dry, dark place for up to six months. Stored shelled nuts in the refrigerator and eat within a few weeks because their high fat content causes them to turn rancid quickly. They are best eaten raw—cooking oxidizes the omega-6 fats.

DID YOU KNOW?

According to research, people who regularly eat nuts are half as likely to have a heart attack as people who never consume them.

MAJOR NUTRIENTS PER 3 TBSP. (1 OZ.) SHELLED BRAZIL NUTS

Calories	197
Protein	4.3 g
Total fat	19.9 g
Carbohydrate	3.7 g
Fiber	2.3 g
Vitamin E	1.7 mg
Calcium	48 mg
Potassium	198 mg
Magnesium	113 mg
Zinc	1.2 mg
Selenium	575 mcg

Oat and nut crunch mix

SERVES 8   (W) (F) (B) (H) (S)

peanut oil, for brushing

1 cup rolled oats

3 tablespoons pine nuts

*¼ cup pistachio nuts
    or hazelnuts*

¼ cup almonds

*¼ cup Brazil nuts,
    coarsely chopped*

2 tablespoons sunflower seeds

2 tablespoons pumpkin seeds

1 tablespoon flaxseeds

⅓ cup chopped dried apricots

⅓ cup golden raisins

1 teaspoon ground cinnamon

Method

1 Heat a nonstick skillet over medium heat and brush with a little oil.
   Add the oats and pine nuts and cook, stirring continuously, for
   8–10 minutes, or until they smell nutty and look a little golden.
   Let cool.

2 Transfer the toasted oat mixture to a large bowl, add all the
   remaining ingredients, and mix together well. Store in an airtight
   container in the refrigerator.

88 HAZELNUTS

Hazelnuts are rich in potassium, a mineral known to reduce fluid retention and lower blood pressure. They also contain cholesterol-lowering plant sterols.

Hazelnuts are high in monounsaturates, which make up 79 percent of their fat content, while their saturated fat content is only 7.5 percent. Monounsaturated fats have been shown to reduce LDL cholesterol and even slightly raise "good" HDL cholesterol. Hazelnuts are also high in beta-sitosterol, a plant fat that can help prevent breast cancer, and which also has cholesterol-lowering action. They are rich in vitamin E, which maintains skin health, heart health, and a healthy immune system, and that may minimize menopausal symptoms, such as hot flashes and poor memory. Vitamin E also works with iron to help keep the red cell count in the blood high. The rich potassium content can help women with high blood pressure, while the magnesium content supports the heart and contributes to bone strength. Hazelnuts are also a good source of soluble fiber, which helps to lower LDL cholesterol.

- Rich in monounsaturates and soluble fiber, both of which help improve blood cholesterol profile.
- Beta-sitosterol, which reduces the risk of breast cancer.
- Vitamin E alleviates menopausal symptoms.

Practical tips:
Hazelnuts keep better than many other types of nut because they contain less polyunsaturated fat and their high vitamin E content acts as a preservative. They go well with butternut squash, dark chocolate, oranges, and pears.

DID YOU KNOW?

Hazelnuts, also called filberts and cobnuts, grow wild in Great Britain, where there is evidence of nut processing as long ago as 9,000 years.

MAJOR NUTRIENTS PER 3 TBSP. (1 OZ.) SHELLED HAZELNUTS

Calories	188
Protein	4.5 g
Total fat	18.2 g
Carbohydrate	5 g
Fiber	2.9 g
Vitamin E	4.5 mg
Niacin	0.5 mg
Vitamin B6	0.16 mg
Folate	34 mcg
Potassium	204 mg
Magnesium	49 mg
Iron	1.4 mg
Zinc	0.7 mg

Zucchini and hazelnut salad with goat cheese

SERMES 4   (W)(B)(H)

4–6 small zucchini, sliced into
*   thin ribbons*
juice of 1 lemon
2 tablespoons olive oil
6–8 basil leaves, coarsely torn
½ cup hazelnuts,
*   toasted and chopped*
2 cups crumbled goat cheese

Method

1 Place the zucchini in a bowl and toss with the lemon juice, olive oil, and basil leaves.

2 To serve, divide among four serving plates and sprinkle with the chopped hazelnuts and crumbled goat cheese.

89 PISTACHIOS

Pistachio nuts are a good addition to the diet during menopause. They are rich in plant sterols, which regulate hormones, and nutrients that keep us healthy.

Pistachio nuts are rich in beta-sitosterols, estrogen-like plant compounds that can help control the typical daily symptoms of menopause, including hot flashes and low mood. Plant sterols can also help lower "bad" LDL blood cholesterol and protect against cancer. They are a good source of fiber, including soluble fiber, which also helps lower LDL blood cholesterol and can help with irritable bowel syndrome (IBS) and constipation. Pistachios are particularly high in the mineral potassium, which can help lower high blood pressure and reduce stomach bloating. High in iron, too, the nuts can prevent anemia and improve energy levels, mood, and brain function. They are a good source of protein, being lower in fat than many other types of nut, and are also one of the few nuts to contain good levels of the eyesight-protective compounds lutein and zeaxanthin.

- Sterols lower blood cholesterol, and may protect against cancer.
- Potassium content lowers blood pressure and eliminates fluid.
- High in fiber and soluble fiber to aid the digestive system and improve blood cholesterol profile.
- Can control blood-sugar levels.

Practical tips:
Pistachios are a luxury nut and as such make an excellent snack. They go well in fruit salads and can also be sprinkled over pasta or rice dishes to serve.

DID YOU KNOW?

Pistachios are one of the few nuts to contain the cancer-preventing compound beta-carotene, which is contained in the green pigment.

MAJOR NUTRIENTS PER 3 TBSP. (1 OZ.) SHELLED PISTACHIOS

Calories	169
Protein	6 g
Total fat	13.5 g
Carbohydrate	8.5 g
Fiber	3 g
Niacin	0.4 mg
Vitamin B6	0.5 mg
Vitamin E	0.7 mg
Calcium	32 mg
Potassium	308 mg
Magnesium	36 mg
Iron	1.2 mg
Zinc	0.7 mg
Lutein/Zeaxanthin	422 mcg

Spicy couscous with pistachios

SERVES 4–6 (F)(H)(M)(S)

1¾ cups couscous

½ teaspoon salt

1¾ cups warm water

1–2 tablespoons olive oil

1–2 tablespoons butter

large pinch of saffron threads

¾ cup blanched almonds

1 cup unsalted pistachio nuts

1–2 teaspoons Ras el hanout
spice mix (available in Middle
Eastern grocery stores, or
subsutitute a mixture of ground
cumin, coriander, and a little
cinnamon)

¾ cup finely sliced dried dates

1 cup finely sliced dried apricots

2 teaspoons ground cinnamon, to
garnish

Method

1 Put the couscous into a bowl. Stir the salt into the water, then pour
over the couscous. Cover and let the couscous absorb the water
for 10 minutes.

2 Drizzle the oil over the couscous. Using your fingers, rub the oil into
the grains to break up the lumps and aerate them.

3 Heat the butter in a heavy skillet, add the saffron, almonds, and
pistachio nuts, and cook for 1–2 minutes, stirring, until the nuts
begin to brown and emit a nutty aroma. Stir in the Ras el hanout,
toss in the dates and apricots, and cook, stirring, for 2 minutes.
Toss in the couscous, mix thoroughly, and heat through.

4 Pile the couscous onto a serving plate in a mound. Garnish with the
cinnamon and serve immediately.

90 PECANS

Pecans are a popular nut in this country. They contain one of the highest levels of plant sterols of all nuts, making them particularly useful during menopause.

If you want to protect your skin, organs, arteries, and bones from aging, eat pecans. They contain many nutrients and phytosterols (plant compounds) that will help you to sail through menopause. Phytosterols are thought to improve the way estrogen is used in our bodies, can lower harmful cholesterol, and protect against breast cancer. Frequent nut consumption is also linked with a lower incidence of type 2 diabetes. As with other nuts, regular pecan eating can assist in weight control, and they are a good source of the minerals known to protect bones, along with the B vitamin thiamin, which supports brain function, and vitamin E and zinc for smoother, healthy skin. Nearly three-quarters of the fat in pecans is oleic acid, the omega-9 fatty acid found also in olive oil. This oil is known to be beneficial to the cardiovascular system because it lowers levels of "bad" LDL cholesterol and maintains or raises "good" HDL cholesterol.

- Contain plant sterols that boost estrogen metabolism and lower blood cholesterol.
- Protect against type 2 diabetes and may help weight control.
- Minerals for bone health and vitamin E and zinc for good skin.

Practical tips:
Pecans are ideal as a snack because they help to keep blood-sugar levels steady. Raw nuts have the most useful compounds. Try adding to fruits as a dessert or sprinkled on salads.

DID YOU KNOW?

You should never eat nuts that smell rancid or have any signs of mold on them; they could be contaminated with poisonous substances called mycotoxins that are dangerous to humans. You can freeze freshly shelled nuts and take them from the freezer as you need them.

MAJOR NUTRIENTS PER ¼ CUP (1 OZ.) SHELLED PECANS

Calories	207
Protein	2.7 g
Total fat	21.6 g
Carbohydrate	4 g
Fiber	2.9 g
Vitamin E	0.4 mg
Thiamin	0.2 mg
Niacin	0.3 mg
Choline	12.2 mg
Potassium	123 mg
Magnesium	36 mg
Calcium	21 mg
Iron	0.8 mg
Zinc	1.4 mg

Pecan- and rice-stuffed mushrooms

SERVES 4

1 tablespoon olive oil

4 scallions, sliced

¼–½ teaspoon crushed, dried
    red pepper

4 large portobello mushrooms

½ cup long-grain rice

3 cups simmering vegetable stock

⅓ cup chopped pecans

⅔ cup grated Manchego cheese

1 tablespoon chopped
    fresh parsley

salt and pepper

Method

1 Preheat the oven to 350°F.

2 Heat the oil in a saucepan and cook the scallions and crushed red pepper for 1–2 minutes.

3 Remove the stems of the mushrooms, chop them, and add to the onion mixture. Cook for 2 minutes. Stir in the rice, then pour in the vegetable stock and bring to a boil. Reduce the heat and simmer for 25 minutes, until the rice is cooked.

4 Place the mushroom caps onto a baking sheet and cook in the preheated oven for 10 minutes.

5 Stir the pecans, Manchego cheese, parsley, and seasoning into the cooked rice, then spoon it over the mushrooms, piling it onto each one. Bake for 10 minutes, then serve immediately.

91 PINE NUTS

Pine nuts are a source of omega-3 fatty acids, which offer a variety of health benefits to women. They also contain protein, vitamin E, zinc, and plant sterols.

These small, soft seeds of the pine tree have a delicate yet distinct flavor. They also have a high fat content, 60 percent of which is polyunsaturated. They contain the omega-3 fatty acid alpha-linolenic acid, which is important for cardiovascular health, and also gamma-linoleic acid, which is linked with an improvement in menopausal symptoms, such as hot flashes, mood swings, and night sweats. These fats may also help improve brain function and help to beat depression. Pine nuts are good sources of vitamin E and zinc, two antioxidants which may increase libido, improve skin condition, and improve heart health. They also contain sterols and stanols, compounds that help lower blood cholesterol and can boost the immune system.

- Polyunsaturated fats may help with menopausal symptoms.
- Contain alpha-linolenic acid and vitamin E for improved heart health.
- Rich in plant sterols for cholesterol-lowering and a stronger immune system.

Practical tips:
Pine nuts make a tasty addition to breakfast cereal and salads, or you can use them as a garnish for soups and vegetable dishes. Try making a fresh basil pesto with basil leaves, pine nuts, grated cheese, and olive oil, and mix with pasta.

DID YOU KNOW?
Pine nuts in the stores may be of several varieties and come from all corners of the world, from the Mediterranean to Asia, as well as the United States. All varieties have similar nutritional benefits.

MAJOR NUTRIENTS PER 2 TBSP. (½ OZ.) PINE NUTS

Calories	101
Protein	2 g
Total fat	10 g
Carbohydrate	2 g
Fiber	0.6 g
Vitamin E	1.4 mg
Potassium	90 mg
Magnesium	38 mg
Iron	0.8 mg
Zinc	1 mg

Spinach, lemon, and pine nut pasta

SERVES 4   (B) (H) (M) (S)

1 pound dried tagliatelle or whole-
*   wheat pasta*
1 cup pine nuts
2 tablespoons olive oil
1 (6-ounce) package baby spinach
grated rind and juice of 1 lemon
pepper
freshly grated Parmesan cheese, to
*   serve (optional)*

Method

1 Cook the pasta in a large saucepan of lightly salted boiling water for 8–10 minutes, or according to the package directions, until the pasta is tender but still firm to the bite. Meanwhile, gently fry the pine nuts in a dry, large skillet until brown.

2 Pour the olive oil over the pine nuts. When the oil is heated, add the spinach leaves. Stir to coat them in the oil, then cover the skillet and let the leaves wilt over medium heat.

3 Drain the pasta, then toss it in the skillet with the pine nuts and spinach. Add the lemon rind and juice and pepper.

4 Serve immediately with grated Parmesan cheese, if using.

92

WALNUTS

Walnuts contain a high level of omega-3 fatty acids and can offer women protection against heart disease, cancers, arthritis, skin complaints, and depression.

Unlike many nuts, walnuts are much richer in polyunsaturated fats than in monounsaturates. These mostly take the form of omega-3 fat alpha-linolenic acid, a special fat that can convert in the body to the essential fats EPA and DHA. An adequate and balanced intake of the omega fats has been linked with protection from aging, cardiovascular disease, cancers, arthritis, skin complaints, and depression, and may help improve brain function. A portion of walnuts a day has also been shown to help protect us in midlife from abdominal fat, which tends to accumulate during this time. The high choline content in the nuts can help to lower dangerous blood homocysteine levels and prevent cardiovascular disease, and may also lower the risk of breast cancer.

- Rich in omega-3 fats and antioxidants for health protection.
- Can help to keep off abdominal fat in midlife.
- Lower cholesterol and blood pressure, helping to prevent heart disease.

Practical tips:
The high levels of polyunsaturated fats in walnuts cause them to turn rancid easily, so they are best stored in the refrigerator. Avoid chopped walnuts because they are not as nutritious. Eat whole walnuts raw as a snack or on your breakfast cereal or yogurt, or pound into a walnut pesto with oil and a little Parmesan cheese.

DID YOU KNOW?

There are numerous species of walnut trees, but the variety from which the nuts are most commonly harvested to eat is Juglans regia, the English walnut—however, it is, in fact, native to India.

MAJOR NUTRIENTS PER 3 TBSP. (1 OZ.) SHELLED WALNUTS

Calories	196
Protein	4.5 g
Total fat	19.5 g
Carbohydrate	4 g
Fiber	2 g
Niacin	0.3 mg
Vitamin B6	0.16 mg
Choline	11.8 mg
Calcium	29 mg
Potassium	132 mg
Magnesium	47 mg
Iron	0.9 mg
Zinc	0.9 mg

Walnut and pecan soda bread

SERVES 4 (B) (H) (M)

3⅔ cups all-purpose flour, plus
  extra for dusting
1 teaspoon baking soda
1 teaspoon cream of tartar
1 teaspoon salt
1 teaspoon sugar
⅓ cup chopped walnuts
⅓ cup chopped pecans
1¼ cups buttermilk

Method

1 Preheat the oven to 350°F. Dust a baking sheet with flour.

2 Sift the flour, baking soda, cream of tartar, and salt into a large mixing bowl. Stir in the sugar and nuts. Pour in the buttermilk and mix to a soft dough.

3 With floured hands, knead the dough briefly on a lightly floured surface, then shape into a circle 8–10 inches in diameter and transfer to the prepared baking sheet. Cut a cross in the top of the dough.

4 Bake in the preheated oven for 30 minutes, then cover with aluminum foil and bake for another 15 minutes.

5 Remove from the oven and let cool slightly. Serve warm in slices.

93 FLAX

Flaxseeds—sometimes called linseeds—are packed full of nutrients. They don't need to be eaten in large quantities to help menopausal health in many ways.

Flaxseeds are rich in alpha-linolenic acid, which the body can partly convert into EPA and DHA, the two forms of omega-3 fatty acid found in oily fish. This essential fatty acid helps to reduce the amount of "bad" LDL cholesterol in the bloodstream and prevent blood clots, and may also improve mood and alleviate depression. The seeds are a good source of choline, a nutrient that can help metabolize fat and may improve memory. Flaxseeds are high in both soluble and insoluble fiber, both of which are essential for good digestive health. They also contain lignans, plant chemicals that have an estrogenic effect and can help minimize hot flashes and night sweats.

- Contains choline, needed to process blood fats and thought to be beneficial for memory.
- Alpha-linolenic acid helps to prevent blood clots and may help to ease depression.
- Lignans reduce hot flashes and night sweats.

Practical tips:
The omega-3 fatty acids in flaxseeds turn rancid easily, so store them in an airtight opaque container in a dark cupboard, and consume within 6–8 weeks. Increase the amount of flaxseeds in your diet by adding them to your breakfast cereal or yogurt, sprinkling them onto green salads and fruit salads, stirring them into a pasta sauce, or sprinkling over vegetables before serving.

DID YOU KNOW?
Research indicates that eating about 1½ tablespoons of flaxseeds a day may significantly reduce the levels of LDL cholesterol in the blood. Daily consumption of flaxseeds may also suppress breast cancer growth.

MAJOR NUTRIENTS PER 1½ TBSP. (½ OZ.) FLAXSEEDS, GOLDEN

Calories	80
Total fat	6.3 g
Protein	2.7 g
Carbohydrate	4.3 g
Fiber	4.1 g
Potassium	122 mg
Calcium	38 mg
Magnesium	59 mg
Iron	0.9 mg
Zinc	0.65 mg
Choline	11.8 mg

Flaxseed and Swiss-style apple muesli

SERVES 2   (W)(B)(H)(M)

1½ cups rolled oats

⅔ cup fresh apple juice
    (not from concentrate)

⅓ cup low-fat milk

½ cup plain yogurt with live cultures

2 small apples, such as Cortland,
    Empire, or Red Delicious, cored
    and grated (leave skin on)

2 teaspons golden flaxseeds

handful of fresh blueberries

6 walnut halves, chopped

Method

1 Put the oats in a mixing bowl and pour over the apple juice. Cover the bowl with plastic wrap and let stand overnight in the refrigerator.

2 Just before serving, stir in the milk, yogurt, grated apple, and flaxseeds. Divide between two serving bowls and top with the blueberries and walnuts.

94

PUMPKIN SEEDS

Pumpkin seeds are rich in sterols, which may protect us against hormone-based cancers. They are also a good source of antioxidant vitamins and minerals.

Pumpkin seeds contain sterols that can encourage the removal of "bad" LDL cholesterol from the body, as well as help to inhibit the development of breast and uterine cancer cells. They are also a good source of significant amounts of minerals, especially zinc and iron. Zinc is an antioxidant that helps to keep the immune system healthy. It also regulates the hormones during the menopausal and postmenopausal years, and so can help to reduce unwanted symptoms, such as hot flashes. Iron is vital for healthy blood cells, energy levels, and brain function. Pumpkin seeds also contain some omega-3 fatty acids, vitamin E, folic acid, and magnesium— all of which can help maintain heart health.

- Contain sterols that protect us against breast and uterine cancers.
- Rich in zinc, supporting hormonal health and the immune system.
- Contain iron for healthy blood and good energy levels.

Practical tips:
These seeds are a great snack. Try adding to a nut mix or stirring into yogurt. They can also be lightly roasted or ground and added to vegetable/nut/bean burgers, or added to bread before baking. If you buy or grow pumpkins, wash and dry the seeds to eat later.

DID YOU KNOW?

Native Americans used pumpkin seeds as both a food and a medicine. During the late nineteenth century, the U.S. pharmacopeia listed pumpkin seeds as an official medicine for the treatment of stomach and digestive problems.

MAJOR NUTRIENTS PER 1 TBSP. (½ OZ.) PUMPKIN SEEDS

Calories	81
Protein	3.7 g
Total fat	6.9 g
Carbohydrate	2.7 g
Fiber	0.6 g
Niacin	0.3 mg
Vitamin E	0.3 mg
Folate	8 mcg
Potassium	121 mg
Magnesium	80 mg
Iron	2.2 mg
Zinc	1.1 mg

Couscous, chickpea, and pumpkin seed pilaf

SERVES 4   (W) (F) (H) (M) (S)

1 cup couscous

1½ cups vegetable stock

1 large yellow bell pepper, seeded and chopped

4 scallions, chopped

10 dried apricots, chopped

⅓ cup golden raisins

½ cup almonds, toasted

½ cup walnut pieces

1 tablespoon pumpkin seeds

¾ cup canned chickpeas, drained and rinsed

2 tablespoons pumpkin seed oil

Method

1 Put the couscous in a large, heatproof bowl. Heat the stock in a saucepan to boiling point, then pour over the couscous and stir well. Cover and let stand for 15 minutes, by which time all the liquid should have been absorbed.

2 Stir all the remaining ingredients, except the oil, into the couscous, forking through lightly. Serve immediately drizzled with the oil.

95

SESAME SEEDS

Sesame seeds help to keep the heart healthy, can ease arthritic pain, relieve skin problems, and boost the libido, so they are extremely valuable during menopause.

Sesame seeds contain two special types of dietary fiber—sesamin and sesamolin—which are members of the lignans group. These fibers are known to help lower harmful LDL cholesterol. Sesame seeds can also lower blood pressure and contain plant sterols, which have a cholesterol-lowering action, too. Other nutrients in sesame seeds include copper, which because of its anti-inflammatory action is thought to reduce the risk of heart disease and the pain of arthritis; iron to help boost memory, and zinc to improve skin quality and libido. Sesame seeds are an important source of calcium for women who don't eat dairy produce, and magnesium, which together help prevent bone loss in midlife.

- Lignans and sterols to help lower cholesterol and high blood pressure.
- Anti-inflammatory, which may reduce arthritis symptoms.
- Good source of bone-building calcium for nondairy eaters.

Practical tips:
Sprinkle the seeds over the top of vegetables, such as broccoli or spinach, before serving, or try adding to grain salads or stirring into cereal. You can also use them to coat homemade breads. Sesame seed paste—tahini—can be bought in health food stores and is a tasty ingredient in hummus.

DID YOU KNOW?

Sesame seeds come in a range of colors, from pale cream through to brown, red, and black. The darker the color, the stronger their flavor tends to be.

MAJOR NUTRIENTS PER 1½ TBSP. (½ OZ.) SESAME SEEDS

Calories	85
Protein	2.5 g
Total fat	7.2 g
Carbohydrate	3.9 g
Fiber	2.5 g
Niacin	0.8 mg
Calcium	20 mg
Potassium	61 mg
Magnesium	52 mg
Iron	1.2 mg
Zinc	1.5 mg

Golden tofu noodles with sesame seeds

SERVES 2 Ⓦ Ⓕ Ⓗ Ⓜ

2 teaspoons virgin coconut oil

⅓ cup tamari

1 tablespoon honey

2-inch piece fresh ginger, finely
   chopped

10 ounces firm tofu, drained,
   patted dry, and cut into
   ½-inch-thick slices

6 ounces soba noodles

1 teaspoon sesame oil

1 carrot, diced

3 radishes, sliced into circles

2 scallions, diagonally sliced

½ cup diagonally sliced snow peas

small handful fresh cilantro leaves,
   chopped

1 teaspoon sesame seeds

pepper

Method

1 Preheat the oven to 375°C. Heat the coconut oil, 3 tablespoons of
   the tamari, the honey, and half of the ginger in a large saucepan
   over medium heat, stirring until combined. Remove from the heat
   and add the tofu, spooning the mixture over until coated, then set
   aside for 10 minutes.

2 Arrange the tofu on a nonstick baking sheet and roast in the
   preheated oven for 20–25 minutes, turning once, until golden.

3 Meanwhile, cook the noodles in a saucepan of gently boiling water
   for 5 minutes, or according to the package directions, until tender.
   Drain, then refresh under cold running water until cool. Transfer to a
   bowl. Mix together the remaining tamari, ginger, and the sesame oil.
   Season with pepper and pour over the noodles.

4 Add the carrot, radishes, scallions, snow peas, and cilantro to the
   noodles. Turn the noodles gently until everything is combined.

5 To serve, divide the noodles between two plates, then scatter the
   sesame seeds over the top and add the tofu.

96

SUNFLOWER SEEDS

Sunflower seeds are rich in vitamin E, which has special benefits during and after menopause. They are also a good source of several other key nutrients.

At around 52 percent total fat, sunflower seeds are higher in fat than most other seeds. Much of this fat takes the form of beneficial polyunsaturates and the essential fat linoleic acid. The remainder is mostly monounsaturates, which offer protection from heart disease. Sunflower seeds are rich in vitamin E, a powerful antioxidant of special importance during the menopausal and postmenopausal years because it helps to slow down the signs of aging, protecting us from heart disease and arthritis and helping preserve skin quality. There is evidence, too, that vitamin E can minimize menopausal symptoms, such as hot flashes and night sweats, poor memory, and vaginal dryness. Sunflower seeds are also rich in plant sterols, which have a cholesterol-lowering effect, and antioxidant minerals, including iron, magnesium, and selenium.

- Rich in the essential fat linoleic acid and a good source of monounsaturated fat.
- High in antioxidant vitamin E, which has a range of health benefits during menopause.
- High in plant sterols that have cholesterol-lowering action.

Practical tips:
The high fat content of sunflower seeds means they spoil quickly and can turn rancid. Keep them somewhere that is cool, dry, and dark. For longer-term storing, they are best frozen. Try adding them to salads, as a snack on their own, or sprinkled on cereal.

DID YOU KNOW?

Sunflower seeds are one of the best sources of vitamin E, containing a whole day's intake in one tablespoon. The vitamin is best supplied to the body in natural form rather than as a supplement, which will be less reliably absorbed.

MAJOR NUTRIENTS PER 1½ TBSP. (½ OZ.) SUNFLOWER SEEDS

Calories	86
Protein	3.4 g
Total fat	7.4 g
Carbohydrate	2.8 g
Fiber	1.6 g
Vitamin E	5.3 mg
Niacin	0.7 g
Folate	34 mcg
Calcium	17 mg
Potassium	103 mg
Magnesium	53 mg
Selenium	8 mcg
Iron	1 mg
Zinc	0.8 mg

Apricot and sunflower seed cookies

MAKES 20   (B) (M)

1 stick unsalted butter, softened

¼ cup demerara sugar or other raw sugar

1 tablespoon maple syrup

1 tablespoon honey, plus extra for brushing

1 extra-large egg, beaten

¾ cup all-purpose flour, plus extra for dusting

1¼ cup whole-wheat flour

1 tablespoon oat bran

½ cup almond meal (ground almonds)

1 teaspoon ground cinnamon

½ cup chopped dried apricots

3 tablespoons sunflower seeds

Method

1 Beat the softened butter with the sugar in a large bowl until light and fluffy. Beat in the maple syrup and honey, then the egg.

2 Add the flours and oat bran, then the almonds and mix well. Add the cinnamon, apricots, and sunflower seeds and, with floured hands, mix to a firm dough. Wrap in plastic wrap and chill for 30 minutes. Preheat the oven to 350°F.

3 Roll out the dough onto a lightly floured surface to ½ inch thick. Using a 2½-inch cookie cutter, cut out 20 circles, rerolling the trimmings where possible, and place on a baking sheet. Brush with a little extra honey and bake in the preheated oven for 15 minutes, until golden. Remove from the oven and let cool on a wire rack.

97

PEANUT OIL

Peanuts are not a true nut but a member of the legume family. The oil is rich in beneficial fats that protect us from the symptoms and diseases of aging.

Peanut oil is high in monounsaturated fats, which help to reduce the risk of heart disease, but it also has a good polyunsaturated content, at around 31 percent, and so contains some omega-3 fatty acids. These can convert in the body to EPA and DHA, the health-protective oils found in oily fish, which are known to benefit heart and brain health and can protect against depression. Because of this good mixture of fats, the oil is ideal for use in cooking at high temperatures because it is less inclined to oxidize—and, therefore, produce aging free radicals—than oils that are high in polyunsaturates. It also contains high levels of plant sterols, particularly coumarins, which are strongly antioxidant and linked with protection from heart disease. The oil is rich in vitamin E, another heart-friendly nutrient that is also linked with a reduction in hot flashes, vaginal dryness, and skin complaints.

- Balance of healthy fats makes it ideal for cooking.
- Contains omega-3 fatty acids, which can improve mood and protect against heart disease and Alzheimer's.
- Vitamin E content may reduce hot flashes.

Practical tips:
Peanut oil is excellent for shallow or deep-frying, roasting, and stir-frying. It can also be used to make mayonnaise or other salad dressings. Cold-pressed oil contains more sterols and vitamin E and has a shorter shelf life. Store in cool, dry, dark conditions.

DID YOU KNOW?

If you choose cold-pressed peanut oil the color will be yellow/amber and the flavor will be sweet and nutty. This oil is particularly suitable for use in salads and to sprinkle over the top of vegetables.

MAJOR NUTRIENTS PER 1 TBSP. (½ FL. OZ.) PEANUT OIL

Calories	119
Total fat	13.5 g
Monounsaturated fat	6.2 mg
Polyunsaturated fat	4.3 mg
Vitamin E	2.2 mg
Plant sterols	28 mg

Wasabi salad dressing

SERVES 4 (W) (H) (M)

3 tablespoons peanut oil

juice of ½ lime

1 teaspoon wasabi paste

1 tablespoon soy sauce

1 teaspoon sesame oil

½ teaspoon dark brown sugar

1 tablespoon rice wine vinegar

Method

1 Beat together all the dressing ingredients in a small bowl, until the sugar has dissolved. This dressing goes particularly well with plain salads that need pepping up.

98 COD LIVER OIL

Used for generations to help maintain healthy joints, cod liver oil provides high levels of essential omega-3 fatty acids, and it is a rich source of vitamins A, D, and E.

Cod liver oil differs from other omega-3 fish oil supplements because it is produced from the fish liver instead of the flesh. Fish liver contains high levels of two essential vitamins: A and D. Vitamin A is important to maintain healthy eyes, eyesight, and healthy skin, while vitamin D—which is hard to find in the average diet—is essential for the absorption of calcium and other minerals in the body. As well as maintaining bone density and preventing osteoporosis, there is evidence that vitamin D can also halt the progress of osteoarthritis. Meanwhile, the omega-3 fatty acids EPA and DHA found in cod liver oil help to maintain supple and flexible joints, as well as a healthy heart and circulation. They can ease the pain of arthritis, lift depression, and improve dry skin, nails, and hair. Cod liver oil contains high levels of vitamin E, which protects against heart disease and may reduce the severity of hot flashes.

- Contains essential fatty acids that promote joint mobility and flexibility and eases joint pain.
- Helps improve the condition of hair, skin, and nails.
- Helps maintain strong, dense bones and teeth.

Practical tips:

Store cod liver oil in the refrigerator to keep it fresh. It is best taken as a supplement. If using cod liver oil in cooking, add it at the last minute; high or prolonged heat destroy the essential fats.

DID YOU KNOW?

Most women obtain much of their vitamin D from sunshine, because the vitamin is produced by the action of sunlight on the skin. In winter months, it is hard to obtain enough.

MAJOR NUTRIENTS PER 1 TBSP. (½ FL. OZ.) COD LIVER OIL

Calories	123
Total fat	13.6 g
EPA	938 mg
DHA	1,500 mg
Vitamin A	13,600 IU
Vitamin D	1,360 IU (34 mcg)
Vitamin E	2.7 mg

Fish stew

SERVES 4–6   (W) (B) (H) (S)

large pinch of saffron threads
¼ cup boiling water
⅓ cup olive oil
1 large onion, chopped
2 garlic cloves, finely chopped
1½ tablespoons chopped
 fresh thyme
2 bay leaves
2 red bell peppers, seeded and
 coarsely chopped
2 (14½-ounce) cans diced
 tomatoes
1 teaspoon sweet smoked paprika
1 cup fish stock
1 cup blanched almonds, toasted
 and finely ground
12–16 mussels, scrubbed and
 debearded
12–16 clams, scrubbed
1¼ pounds thick, boned hake or
 cod fillets, skinned and cut into
 2-inch chunks
12–16 shrimp, heads and tails
 removed, deveined
1 tablespoon cod liver oil
salt and pepper
thick crusty bread, to serve

Method

1 Put the saffron in a heatproof bowl, add the water, and set aside to steep.

2 Heat the oil in a large, heavy flameproof casserole dish over medium–high heat. Reduce the heat to low, add the onion, and sauté for 10 minutes, until golden, but not brown. Stir in the garlic, thyme, bay leaves, and bell peppers and cook for another 5 minutes, or until the peppers are soft. Add the tomatoes and paprika and continue to simmer for 5 minutes, stirring frequently.

3 Stir in the stock, reserved saffron water, and ground almonds and bring to a boil,

stirring frequently. Reduce the heat and simmer for 5–10 minutes, until the sauce reduces and thickens. Season with salt and pepper.

4 Meanwhile, prepare the mussels and clams. Discard any with broken shells and those that do not close when tapped.

5 Gently stir in the hake so it doesn't break up and add the shrimp, mussels, and clams. Reduce the heat to low, cover the casserole dish, and simmer for 3 minutes then add the cod liver oil. Cook for another 2 minutes, or until the hake is cooked through, the shrimp have turned pink, and the mussels and clams have opened; discard any mussels or clams that remain closed. Serve at once with plenty of thick, crusty bread for soaking up the juices.

99

HEMP SEED OIL

Hemp seed oil contains a perfect balance of omega-6 to omega-3 fatty acids, along with gamma-linolenic acid (GLA), which can help alleviate menopausal symptoms.

Hemp seed oil is the only oil to contain what experts believe is a perfect balance for human health of omega-6 and omega-3 fatty acids—a ratio of 3:1. It is an exceptionally rich source of linoleic acid (omega-6) and alpha-linolenic acid (omega-3), which are vital for the prevention or control of a variety of conditions common in midlife, including heart disease, cancers, arthritis, and painful joints, and skin complaints. Omega-3s are particularly linked with the prevention of memory loss, optimal brain function, the easing of depression, and a reduction in cardiovascular disease. Hemp seed oil also contains some GLA, a fatty acid that is renowned for its ability to help balance female hormones and aid nerve function, and oleic acid, an omega-9 fatty acid that can help heart health.

- Unique balanced source of omega-6 and omega-3 fatty acids.
- Provides a range of important health benefits during menopause, midlife, and old age.
- Contains GLA for hormone balancing and oleic acid, along with a small amount of vitamin E, for heart health.

Practical tips:
Use as a salad/vegetable dressing, either on its own or combined with other ingredients. Or try blending it with your morning smoothie. Store in the refrigerator and don't use it for cooking; some of the beneficial nutrients may be lost and the oils may oxidize. A typical daily intake for health protection is 1 tablespoon.

DID YOU KNOW?

Hemp seeds do not contain tetrahydrocannabinol (THC), the drug that is the psychoactive substance in marijuana/cannabis, the hemp plant. Minute amounts of THC may be transferred from the leaves into the oil during pressing. However, these trace amounts are too low to have any effects.

MAJOR NUTRIENTS PER 1 TBSP. (½ FL. OZ.) HEMP SEED OIL

Calories	123
Total fat	13.6 g
Linoleic acid (omega-6)	7.75 g
Alpha-linolenic acid (omega-3)	2.5 g
GLA	340 mg
Vitamin E	20 mg

Grapefruit and fennel salad

SERVES 4–6   (**H**) (**M**) (**S**)

2 ruby or pink grapefruit

1 teaspoon salt

1 fennel bulb

2–3 scallions, thinly sliced

1 teaspoon cumin seeds

2 tablespoons hemp seed oil

1 tablespoon olive oil

handful of ripe black olives,
    to garnish

Method

1 Using a knife, remove and discard the rind from the grapefruit and cut down between the membranes to remove the segments intact, discarding any seeds. Cut each segment in half, put in a bowl, and sprinkle with the salt.

2 Cut the fennel bulb in half lengthwise, then crosswise, and finely slice with the grain.

3 Add to the grapefruit and toss in the scallions, cumin seeds, and oils. Garnish the salad with olives and serve.

100 OLIVE OIL

Consumed in the Mediterranean region for thousands of years, health-giving olive oil is now cherished worldwide for its protective properties.

Olive oil is perhaps the healthiest fat you can eat. Its main fatty acid is omega-9, oleic acid, and it has a higher monounsaturated fat content than any other oil. These fats are known for their cholesterol-lowering ability, which, in turn, reduces our risk of heart disease and stroke. Virgin olive oils also contain a range of antioxidant plant compounds, including: hydroxytyrosol and oleuropein, which can protect against breast cancer and high blood pressure; lignans, which can also lower cholesterol and may protect against cancers; oleocanthal, which is anti-inflammatory; and quercetin, which stimulates the cells to repair themselves and helps hold back the signs of aging. It is a good source of vitamin K, too, which helps protect us against osteoporosis, and the antioxidant vitamin E, which keeps skin supple, improves libido and brain function, and reduces the severity of hot flashes.

- Improves blood cholesterol profile.
- Protects against breast cancer and osteoporosis and fights the signs of aging.
- Vitamin E can help minimize several menopausal symptoms.

Practical tips:
Store in the dark because light destroys the plant compounds it contains. Use within a month or two of buying. Extra virgin olive oil is best used as it is, instead of heated. Serve it as a dip, drizzle it over vegetables, or use in salad dressings.

DID YOU KNOW?

The best olive oil to choose for health is extra virgin olive oil, preferably cold-pressed. It contains much higher levels of the sterols and other compounds than highly refined olive oil.

MAJOR NUTRIENTS PER 1 TBSP. (½ FL. OZ.) OLIVE OIL

Calories	132
Total fat	15 g
Monounsaturated fat	4.62 g
Omega-9 fatty acids	10,689 mg
Vitamin E	2.15 mg
Vitamin K	8.1 mcg

Pesto sauce

SERVES 4 (**W**) (**B**) (**H**)

40 fresh basil leaves

3 garlic cloves, crushed

3 tablespoons pine nuts

½ cup finely grated
   Parmesan cheese

2–3 tablespoons extra virgin
   olive oil

salt and pepper

Method

1 Rinse the basil leaves and pat them dry with paper towels. Put the basil leaves, garlic, pine nuts, and Parmesan cheese into a food processor or blender and process for 30 seconds, or until smooth. Alternatively, pound all of the ingredients in a mortar with a pestle.

2 If you are using a food processor, keep the motor running and slowly add the olive oil. Alternatively, add the oil drop by drop while stirring briskly. Season with salt and pepper.

GLOSSARY

Alpha-linolenic acid An omega-3 polyunsaturated fatty acid, which the body can convert into EPA and DHA. It is essential for health and must come from the diet because our bodies can't manufacture it.

Amino acids The 22 "building blocks" of protein that are contained in many foods in varying combinations and amounts. Nine of the 22 are essential and we can derive them only from food.

Anthocyanin A purple, red, or blue pigment in certain foods; a powerful antioxidant.

Antioxidant Substance that protects the body against the harmful effects of free radicals, toxins, and pollutants.

Beta-carotene See carotenes.

Beta-cryptoxanthin/ cryptoxanthin Strong antioxidant with an ability to reduce the risk of certain cancers.

Beta-glucan A type of soluble fiber found in certain plants.

Beta-sitosterol Plant sterol that reduces blood cholesterol.

Bioflavonoid/flavonoid A group of several thousand antioxidant compounds.

Carotenes/carotenoids Yellow, red, and orange pigments that have several health benefits. The main types are alpha- and beta-carotene. Lutein, lycopene, and zeaxanthin are others.

Catechin A compound from the flavonoid group, found in tea and certain other plants, which can help protect against cardiovascular disease.

Cholesterol A fatty substance present in many foods of animal origin and manufactured in humans in the liver. It is essential in the body, but under certain circumstances can also encourage the development of coronary artery disease. See also HDL and LDL.

Coumestrol Plant compound with estrogen-like effects; it is also anti-inflammatory, helping prevent arthritis, heart disease, and cancers.

Cyanidin Anti-inflammatory plant chemical that can help to relieve the symptoms of arthritis and gout, and offers heart disease and cancer protection.

Daidzein A plant isoflavone that has mild estrogen-like effects.

DHA Docosahexaenoic acid An omega-3 fatty acid found in oily fish with several health benefits, such as in the prevention of cardiovascular disease, to aid brain power, and to minimize depression.

Diabetes A condition where the amount of glucose in your blood is too high. Type 1 diabetes is when no insulin (vital to help the body use glucose for energy) is produced by the pancreas; type 2 diabetes is when only some is produced, or when the insulin that is produced does not work properly.

Ellagic acid A polyphenol antioxidant with anticancer properties.

EPA Eicosapentaenoic acid An omega-3 fatty acid found in oily fish with several health benefits, such as in the prevention of cardiovascular disease and to aid brain power and minimize depression.

Essential fatty acid/essential fat/EFA Essential polyunsaturated fats that our bodies need for health, which must be provided in the diet. The essential omega-6 fat is linoleic acid, the essential omega-3 fat is alpha-linolenic acid.

Estrogen A female hormone produced by the ovaries. After menopause, estrogen levels decline sharply and this decline is linked with problems, including osteoporosis, reduction in libido, and increased risk of heart disease.

Flavonoid See bioflavonoid.

Free radical Highly reactive, unstable atoms or molecules in the body that are a normal by-product of metabolism but are believed, in excess, to be a factor in onset of disease and aging.

Genistein See daidzein.

Glycemic index A system of ranking carbohydrate foods according to their effect on blood-sugar levels. A rank of 100, the rating for sugar, is the highest. Type 2 diabetics need to follow a low glycemic index diet for best control of the disease.

HDL High-density lipoproteins that bind to cholesterol and carry it through the blood. Sometimes called "good" cholesterol because it may keep arteries clear and protect against cardiovascular disease.

Homocysteine An amino acid that is synthesized in our bodies, high levels of which in the blood are a strong risk factor for cardiovascular disease.

Hydroxycinnamic acids Antioxidants that boost the good bacteria in the digestive tract and help prevent digestive disorders.

Immune system Processes within the body that protect against disease and other potentially harmful pathogens.

Indoles Plant compounds that have strong anticancer activity.

Insulin A hormone produced by the pancreas that regulates blood-sugar levels.

Insulin resistance A condition occuring in type 2 diabetes, when the insulin doesn't work effectively and it builds up in the blood.

Inulin A type of carbohydrate that acts as dietary fiber and a prebiotic in our digestive systems.

Irritable bowel syndrome (IBS) A digestive system disorder characterized most commonly by cramping, abdominal pain, bloating, constipation, and diarrhea.

LDL Low-density lipoproteins that transport fats, such as cholesterol, in the blood. High levels of LDL cholesterol are linked with cardiovascular disease. Sometimes called "bad" cholesterol.

Lignan A type of plant estrogen.

Limonene Antioxidant oil that appears to help prevent breast cancer. It may also help to lower LDL blood cholesterol.

Linoleic acid A type of omega-6 polyunsaturated fatty acid that is essential for human health and must come from the diet as our bodies cannot manufacture it.

L-tyrosine/tyrosine An amino acid that can help improve brain function and energy levels.

Lutein See carotenes.

Lycopene A type of carotene that can help prevent cancer.

Metabolic syndrome A cluster of symptoms becoming increasingly common in midlife, consisting of high waist circumference denoting interabdominal fat, insulin resistance, impaired glucose tolerance, high blood pressure, and poor blood fat profile.

Metabolism The chemical reactions that happen in the body to maintain life, during which food and drink are broken down and their nutrients used for body repair, maintenance, and energy.

Monounsaturated fatty acids/fats A type of fat that has a beneficial effect on cholesterol levels, cardiovascular disease, and other health problems.

Omega-3 Types of polyunsaturated fat that are vital for normal body functioning, have a range of health benefits, and protect against a variety of diseases.

ORAC The oxygen radical absorbance capacity, which is an international method of measuring the antioxidant effect of plant foods, according to their capacity to neutralize free radicals.

Pectin A type of soluble fiber whose health benefits include a reduction in blood LDL levels.

Phenolic compound/phenol/polyphenol Group of antioxidant plant compounds, which are strongly linked with the prevention of heart disease.

Phytochemical/phytonutrient Chemical compounds found in plants that are known to have health benefits, but that are different from vitamins and minerals.

Polyunsaturated Type of fat, usually high in omega-6 fatty acids. Omega-3s are a less abundant type of polyunsaturated fat.

Prebiotics Compounds, called oligosaccharides, that stimulate the growth of beneficial bacteria in the intestines.

Probiotics "Friendly" bacteria, such as acidophilus and bifidobacteria, that help boost the immune system.

Pterostilbene Compound that helps inhibit the oxidation of LDL cholesterol, and keeps arteries healthy.

Quercetin An antioxidant found in tea, onions, and apples.

Rutin Compound that strengthens veins and may help prevent varicose and thread veins and minimize fluid retention.

Saponins Plant compounds that have been shown to inhibit tumor growth and are found in legumes.

Soluble fiber A type of dietary fiber that can have a beneficial effect on digestive health and cholesterol levels.

Sterols/plant sterols/phytosterols Plant compounds that can have a cholesterol-lowering effect in the body.

Sulfides/organosulfides Antioxidant and immune-stimulating compounds.

Sulforaphane A plant compound that has anticancer and antidiabetic properties.

Tannins Plant compounds from the polyphenol group that can inhibit the absorption of minerals but that can have some health protection effects.

Tryptophan Amino acid that enables relaxation and improves mood by promoting the secretion of the brain chemical serotonin.

Zeaxanthin See carotenes.

INDEX